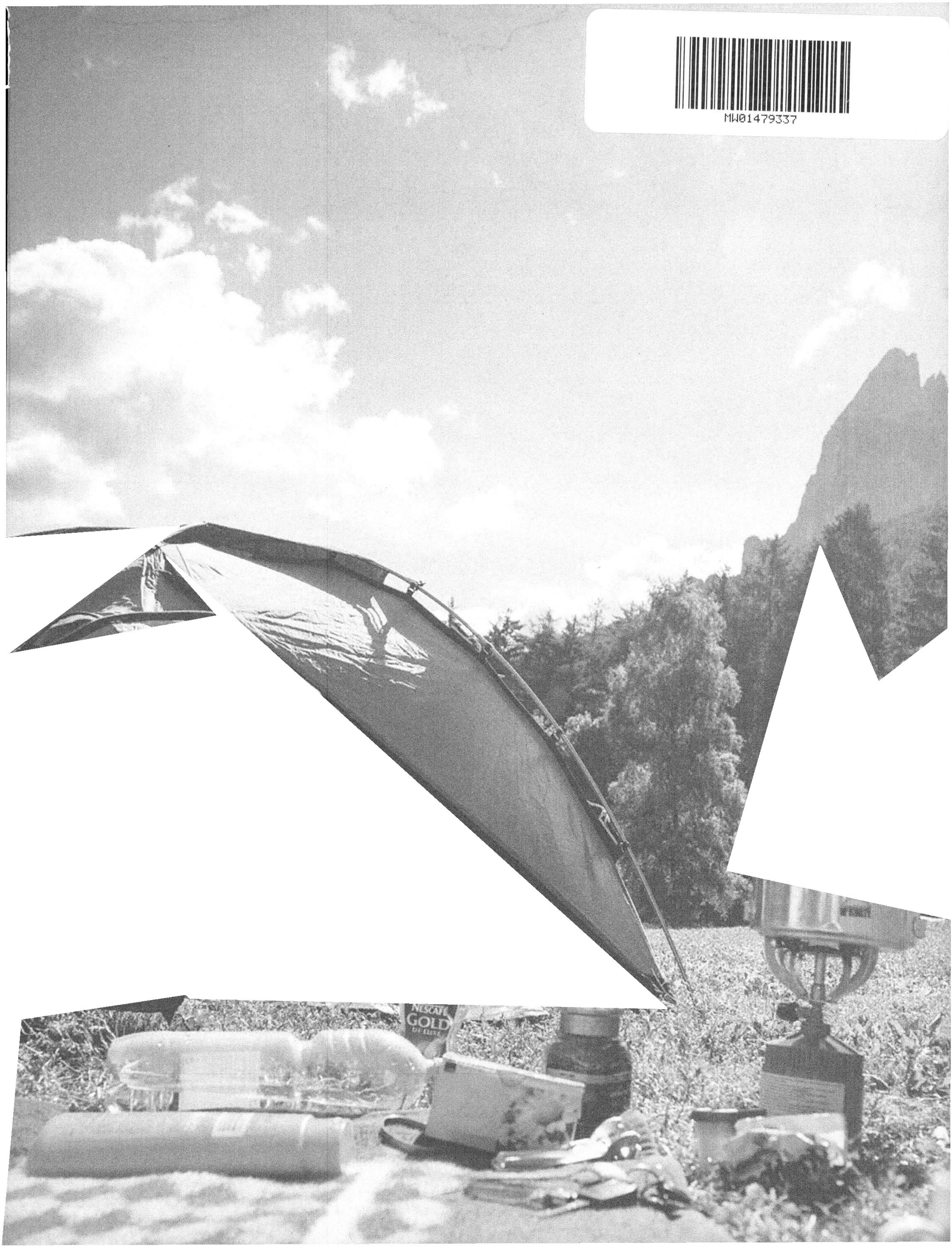
NESCAFÉ
GOLD

CAMPING COOKBOOK

The Easiest and Most Delicious Recipes for Gourmet Outdoor Cooking with Cast Iron Skillets over Campfires with Family and Friends

By

Albert Franklin

INFINITY PRESS

Camping Cookbook

Copyright - 2021 -

All rights reserved. The content contained within this book may not be reproduced, duplicated or transmitted without direct written permission from the author or the publisher. Under no circumstances will any blame or legal responsibility be held against the publisher, or author, for any damages, reparation, or monetary loss due to the information contained within this book. Either directly or indirectly. Legal Notice: This book is copyright protected. This book is only for personal use. You cannot amend, distribute, sell, use, quote or paraphrase any part, or the content within this book, without the consent of the author or publisher. Disclaimer Notice: Please note the information contained within this document is for educational and entertainment purposes only. All effort has been executed to present accurate, up to date, and reliable, complete information. No warranties of any kind are declared or implied. Readers acknowledge that the author is not engaging in the rendering of legal, financial, medical or professional advice. The content within this book has been derived from various sources. Please consult a licensed professional before attempting any techniques outlined in this book. By reading this document, the reader agrees that under no circumstances is the author responsible for any losses, direct or indirect, which are incurred as a result of the use of information contained within this document, including, but not limited to, - errors, omissions, or inaccuracies.

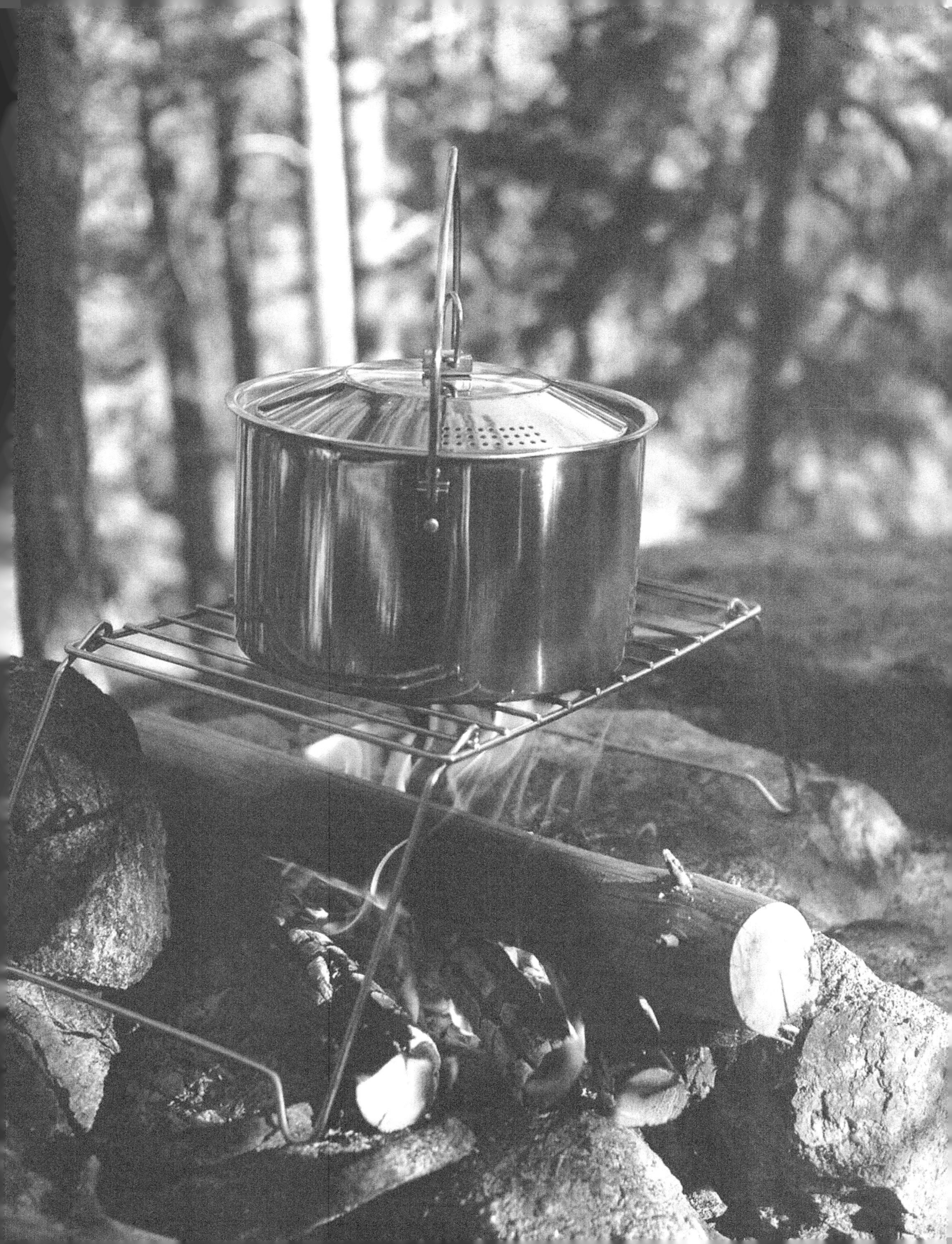

Camping Cookbook

Table of Contents

Introduction 8

Chapter 1. Skillet 9

Chapter 2. How to Build the Perfect Campfire? 15

Chapter 3. Three Crucial Campfire 20

Chapter 4 Do's and Don'ts 25

Chapter 5. Type of Cooking Pie Iron 28

Chapter 6. Car Camping 31

Chapter 7. Breakfast 33

Chapter 8. Lunch and Dinner 51

Chapter 9. Soups and Stews 77

Chapter 10. Snacks and Sides 89

Camping Cookbook

Chapter 11. Desserts and Drinks 102

Chapter 12. Backcountry Camping 116

Chapter 13. Breakfast 118

Chapter 14. Lunch and Dinner 140

Chapter 15. Snacks and Sides 152

Chapter 16. Desserts and Drinks 167

Conclusion 177

Introduction

Camping would help you to enjoy the beauty of our mother nature, and you can have plenty of fresh air as well. You don't need plenty of stuffs for camping.

Camping presents a special opportunity for the inner kid to bond, reigniting the creative spirit broken down by the daily grind. Children excel on a holiday's liberty and adventure where the daily schedule is thrown aside, and no one nags them about personal grooming. It's also a wonderful chance to give them some accountability, which the independence they will enjoy will richly reward them. If you're going to enjoy the experience of hiking completely, it's best to leave the urban world as far as possible at home. Whether you're struggling to get a Wi-Fi link and pick-up work emails, or you cut short the campfire chatter to go inside and watch television, it's hard to reconnect with nature.

You don't need any special day or occasion to go and spend a day or two outside with your friends or even family. Camping not only recharges your batteries, but it improves the quality of your life as well. You would feel more optimistic, balanced, and energized.

If you haven't planned the trip yet then, go for it, and this book would help you with the delicious recipes that you can try there.

This book has all in it, which one could forget while preparing for the trip but having this book in hand would not let it happen. How? The answer is that one could get a list of all the necessary tools or stuff, such as; torch, tent, pots, lighter, insect repellent, sanitizer, first aid kit, cooler, and many other camping related things along with them. One could check it in the given list, whether they are missing anything or not.

Besides, this book has various kinds of recipes that would be easy to make while camping and not wasting most of the time cooking and not appreciating nature's beauty. This book covers recipes regarding breakfast, lunch, dinner, and even snacks. It also contains recipes catering to the sweet tooth as well. Having prepared snacks with you would save time and let you enjoy and relax, away from all kinds of pollution. Overall, it is a guide for everyone, containing all the details you need to focus on while planning and preparing ahead and not forgetting anything.

Chapter 1. Skillet

This vessel is a very helpful tool when it comes to cooking outdoors. Many campers opt to use a cast-iron skillet because of its durability and its ability to preserve heat. Aside from this, you won't have to use a lot of oil because of its natural non-stick properties. Because of this, it's also a lot easier to clean because the cooked food slides right off. This vessel is great for fried meals cooked over the campfire, hot coals, or a portable camping stove.

CAST IRON CARE

Properly seasoned and well-cared-for cast iron cookware can last for generations. It can also continue to function as an easy-release surface far longer than modern coated nonstick pans. However, the key is proper maintenance, and that's where cast iron cookware incites endless debate and anxiety. Everyone knows that cast iron cookware requires maintenance, but what does that mean exactly? So intense is the fear of doing it wrong that some people simply don't use their cast iron cookware at

Camping Cookbook

all, letting it idle aimlessly in the cupboard. This section offers all the information you need to care for and maintain your cast iron skillet properly.

Seasoning a New Skillet

Seasoning is a natural way to give your cast iron cookware a nonstick coating. In simple terms, seasoning means coating the pan with oil and then heating it. This causes the fat to bond to the surface of the pan, giving it a nonstick coating.

The more complicated explanation involves a bit of science. A new cast iron pan will have many tiny cracks, pores, and other surface irregularities. If you cook food in the pan when it is in this state, the food will stick because it will seep into these nooks and crannies.

Furthermore, due to chemical reactions, proteins in the food will actually bond with the metal causing—you guessed it!—sticking. So, the answer is to fill in these little imperfections and create a protective layer between the pan and the food.

If you purchase a new cast iron pan, the box will likely proclaim that it is "pre-seasoned," so you can cook with it right away, but I strongly recommend that you re-season it if you have the time. A good, thick layer of seasoning takes several applications to build.

Cleaning Your Cast Iron

There is a lot of debate about the right way to clean cast iron. The truth is that several methods work well, and different levels of mess can call for different tricks. I've included what I've found to be the five most foolproof methods here. One rule you should always adhere to: clean your cast iron skillet immediately after use.

- *Hot water.* This is by far the simplest and most common cleaning method. If your skillet is well seasoned, food particles should come right off with just a bit of elbow grease, some hot water, and a sponge or a stiff, natural—or plastic-bristle (not wire) brush.

- *Boiling water.* If you're having trouble removing stuck-on food, rinse the skillet while it is still hot. Fill the skillet again and bring the water to a boil. Boil for a few minutes to break up stuck-on food. Use a spatula to dislodge food residue, lightly scraping the bottom and sides of the pan. Be careful to do this gently so that you don't scrape off the pan's seasoning layers.

Camping Cookbook

- ***Kosher salt.*** If you are still left with lots of stuck-on food residue, make a paste of coarse kosher salt and warm water and use it as a scrub to scour off stuck-on food.

- ***A raw potato.*** Cut a raw potato in half and dip the cut side into either soap or baking soda. Use the potato's cut side to scrub the skillet well, slicing off the surface and adding more soap or baking soda as needed. This cleaning method is especially effective for ridding your skillet of rust.

When you have finished cleaning and drying your skillet, heat the pan briefly over medium heat and then rub a lightly oil-soaked paper towel over the interior of the skillet. Wipe again with a clean paper towel to remove any excess oil. Allow the pan to cool, and store in a dry place.

Camping Cookbook

DUTCH OVEN

The Dutch oven is basically a heavy container pot with a tight-fitting lid.

This cast iron pot may look like an outdoor cooking appliance, but in reality, it can also be a gift to home chefs around the world. In a Dutch oven, you can cook almost anything.

We're talking about one-pot meals, such as Alfredo pasta and tomato sauces, soups, sandwiches, biscuits, chili, beef stew, casserole, and the preparation of individual ingredients, such as sauces and garnishes.

You can even cut down on cooking time with a Dutch oven because the pot can go straight into the oven from the stovetop without missing a beat, and you can put all of your ingredients in one bowl for many Dutch oven recipes.

If you're looking for an outdoor Dutch oven, examine the bail handle. It should have a heavy gauge wire on the oven side and be firmly connected to shaped tangs. Avoid ovens that have riveted tabs.

Most of the oven handles lie in both directions against the side of the oven, but with close examination, you can find some with a handle that stands at an angle of 45 degrees on one leg.

The handle on the lid should also be carefully examined. There should be a loop attached to both ends of the cover, and it should be hollow in the center for easy locking. Stay away from those with a sturdy shaped tab for a handle on the door.

An improper lid will be very difficult to grasp and handle, especially when using a lot of coal. The loop layout offers much better control. The lid should have a lip or ridge around the outer edge.

Finally, look for a second handle attached to the lid or top rim at the oven base.

Many ovens are available with a handle of the skillet type attached to the lid. This is a good idea in theory, but in fact, it seems that they are more in the way and don't provide adequate support.

These handles also get in the way during storage and packaging. It is essential to avoid fixed handles on the oven base, although I believe the theory behind these handles was to promote the placement of the oven in a deep fireplace.

Take a couple of red bricks with you to the store and put them in an oven with this type of handle. Then try to raise the pot with the handle, and you'll see that the handle is useless. A loaded oven can be a real wrist-breaker, weighing 20 to 25 lbs.

Camping Cookbook

Aluminum tends to heat quicker, taking less preheating time, but it does not hold the heat for long after removing it from the coals. Because aluminum also reflects more heat than cast iron, it will take more coals to reach a set temperature and sustain it.

DUTCH OVEN TYPES

Camping: these Dutch ovens have three legs to keep the coals off, a wire bail handle, and a slightly concave, rimmed cover to place the coals or briquettes on top and bottom. It makes internal heat more consistent and allows the inside to act as an oven. Usually, these ovens were made of bare cast iron.

Modern: these Dutch ovens are designed to be used on the stove or in the oven and usually have a lipless top. Like the unglazed ovens, many older types retained the handle, while others, like the enameled, had two handles of the ring. Traditional Dutch ovens consist of cast iron, cast aluminum, or ceramic.

SELECTING/BUYING A DUTCH OVEN

Camping Dutch ovens are usually bought from hardware stores or sporting goods shops. New Dutch ovens can be sold in supermarkets or in cooking supply shops for the stovetop or traditional oven.

Camping Cookbook

Determine the size, style as well as form needed when buying a Dutch oven. The Dutch aluminum oven is popular with backpackers as it is lighter, rustproof and does not need to be seasoned.

If you choose an aluminum oven, be careful not to overheat the oven because this can permanently damage the pan. Many people prefer cast iron ovens because they heat more uniformly and remain hot longer. Typically, the cost is about the same.

Choose the Dutch oven that best suits your needs. Dutch ovens are also available in various sizes and use a size numbering system. The table below shows the various size, weight and capacity.

Diameter	*Weight*	Capacity	Serving Capacity
8"	3 lbs.	2 quarts	2-4 people
10"	5.5 lbs.	4 quarts	4-6 people
12"	7.5 lbs.	6 quarts	6-10 people
14"	9.5 lbs.	8 quarts	10-12 people
16"	11 lbs.	10 quarts	13-15 people
18"	13 lbs.	12 quarts	16-18 people
20"	14.5 lb.	14 quarts	19-22 people

Chapter 2. How to Build the Perfect Campfire?

HOW TO BUILD A CAMP FOR COOKING?

The purpose is to convert all wood to coal at the same time. This can produce uniform flame, not burning flame or burning black cookware. It can also get the longest cooking time from coal.

Prepare the Site

Choose a source of fire of at least 8' from the bushes or any combustible materials. Make sure there are no hanging branches in the scene.

Use large stones or green stems to create a U-shaped circumference. If you use records, you need to check them from time to time. If the breeze blows, please face the wind behind the campfire.

A large stone is placed behind the stove as a chimney. "Chimney Rock" will help smoke and getaway.

Lay the Kindling

Fill the fire area with wrinkled paper or a fire.

Lay it down on the paper layer with the layer, each layer switching direction. Use chopped wood or small dry branches. Do not place the "conical tent pattern." The fire area must be completely covered with lighted chimneys.

Place a bucket of water near the fire zone. Turn the leaf to light a fire.

Build a Fire, Grade the Coals

When lit, add firewood. Wood should be as large as possible. Use solid or hard branches (if any). Distribute the wood evenly over the fire bed.

After the last flame has been extinguished, most of the remainder is white coal. Please use a stick to push the charcoal to the back end's top position and push the front end's bottom position to it. This will provide you with "Hi," "Med," and "Low" cooking settings. Or, iron the charcoal according to your preference.

For cooking, place the grill on the rocks or the damp green tree trunks. Place food directly on the grill or cooking utensils and prepare meals. If you cook directly on the grill, you can use a small spray bottle or spray gun to extinguish the rogue flame that usually occurs due to food distillation.

When the fire weakens, the coal is accumulated to get the most heat from it.

After cooking, add wood to the campfire at night. Before retiring, quench well and soak it in water. Place the stone on the fire bed. If necessary, it can be easily reassembled the next day.

WHAT WOOD TO USE, DETERMINE THE TEMPERATURE OF THE FIRE AND TRICKS

Cooking in a campfire requires clean, burning fire. This can only be done with dried and marinated wood. Trees that strip green woods in vain-fire can smoke, burn badly, and cause unnecessary pollution. If there is no dry wood, then it must be filled. Firewood is available in many public camps–please contact available firewood.

Ash

Fraxinus Mandshurica, or the most common ash, is the Yuleaceae family tree. There are about 50 different species, some are evergreen, and others are rough. Ash is considered one of the best firewood in the world. It burns easily, maintains very little moisture, and does not produce much smoke. These properties make them very suitable for use in campfires. Unlike other woods, white wax burns when it is green. If you find some ash around the camp, try burning it.

Cedar

If you want to build a burning fire to keep it warm, look for flammable cedarwood. The flame it produces is not as large as some other woods mentioned above, but it lacks the flame's size and is made of heat. Cedar produces excellent heat and is ideal for burning wood on cold nights. In addition, the cedar has a unique and pleasant aroma, which is not found anywhere else. Most people love this hidden and unique perfume. Of course, that's why some furniture polishes and other consumer products carry the scent of cedar.

The only drawback to beech is that it is heavy and takes some time to burn completely.

Black Cherry

Black cherry has low smoke and a unique aroma, which is easy to handle wood and is very suitable for different campsites. It provides moderate heat and cool sparks, so it is best to choose wood in summer or spring. You just need a gentle breeze to catch up with, and its lovely scent makes it perfect for you to smoke a piece of meat, fish or chicken in the camp kitchen.

Black cherry cannot provide the heat and light that other types of wood (such as beech) can provide, so it is not ideal for winter adventures.

DETERMINE THE TEMPERATURE OF THE FIRE

Internal temperature: fire can reach an internal temperature of 1650 °F (900 °C) in a flame, which is called a continuous flame region.

Cooking temperature: above the flame where the flame is not visible (called the hot column region); the temperature can be expected to be around 600° F (320° C). This is where you cook. The further away from the flame, the lower the temperature.

Large campfires (such as campfires) may get hotter–more than 2,000 degrees Fahrenheit (1,100 °C). Of course, you are not likely to cook over a full-size campfire.

A typical campfire will become hot enough to melt aluminum cans, but not a cast-iron frying pan.

You may have seen what happens when you put a soda can (aluminum alloy) in the fire–it will almost melt and disappear, except for the top and bottom parts of the soda can.

Camping Cookbook

VARIABLES AFFECTING THE CAMPFIRE TEMPERATURE

- Like all fires, the temperature varies with many factors.
- Fuel type: wood type (softwood, hardwood and resin) and dry (sun-dried or green).
- Fire size: the amount of fuel will affect the degree of fire.
- Oxygen flow: the fire in a metal fire pit will not be at the same temperature as the fire with the continuous oxygen supply (a breeze or a blower pair).
- A good fire contains three components: fuel, air, and heat. Long flammable fires are hotter to burn than well-prepared and stable fires, and this is what we do for cooking.

INGREDIENTS TO A GOOD FIRE

You will need three things:

1. Tinder: small branches, dead leaves, etc., will quickly ignite and generate heat, and begin to burn more wood. Paper, cardboard, and flaming agents can also be used as a fire.
2. Kindle: a thicker wooden block that is easier to burn than the log block you placed on it. These branches can be larger, thicker, small branches or pieces of primary fuel, which peel off larger trunks. When it burns quickly, you will start to produce charcoal, which lays a good foundation for your fire.
3. Fuel: the larger and tougher wood that is placed on top usually requires more heat and flame to burn, but once it is burned, it will burn, which is an ideal fire for cooking.

For cooking, you need heat to cook steadily as it does at home. If you stack everything up and create a fiery hell at once, it might look impressive, but it's not perfect for cooking.

Heavy fire can reach 1650° F (900° C), and aluminum can melt–it will quickly chew wood supplies and burn food.

Camping Cookbook

In order to cook, your fire must burn first and then create uniform coal.

Start with Tinder. The tin can heat up and ignite, and when it burns, it will generate enough heat for your bulk fuel.

When it burns, it resembles the top of the burner, forming an ideal uniform heat source, and you can change the temperature by adding more records.

Camping Cookbook

Chapter 3.Three Crucial Campfire

Camping Cookbook

SNACK FIRE

Sometimes, you just need enough fire to heat a cup of coffee or fry it in the afternoon. Or, it might not have been a temporary facility for a permanent camp. You don't want the fire to be too big, so cleaning upon departure will waste a lot of time. Enter the snack fire. Snack fires are just basic tent fires. It is small but very effective.

To build it, just move the branches close together, so a small conical tent is formed. Place an open space in the center where the fire can be placed. Newspaper balls, dried leaves, and dried pine needles work better. By practice, you can shoot in seconds. In order for the fire to continue spreading, please continue to add small branches on the floor.

To brew coffee or bacon roasted with boiling water, wait until the conical tent has fallen before placing the frying pan or kettle in the middle. Continue adding small branches around the pot to increase the heat.

COOKING FIRE

Cooking on an outside cooking fire when you plan to stay somewhere for more than a day and want to build a serious fire, you should build a cooking fire. Campers often try to cook by placing pots and pans directly on a fire. However, this usually leads to unsatisfactory results in burning utensils and food. This caused some handbags to walk along with the camping stove, but you can use all-natural materials to make an effective fireplace.

First, set up the fire near the tent. Make it larger than snacks. When you are on fire, put two other records side by side, about 7 inches at one end and about 4 inches at the other end. These two stems are used as a stove where you can put pots and pans. You can place a narrower bowl like a coffee bowl on the narrower end and a larger bowl on the wider end. This allows you to cook many dishes at the same time. Distribute or stack coal to form hotter or cooler cooking areas.

If you want to make it more accurate, you can put a pole on the fire. After that, you can hang the pan a few inches above the fire to cook carefully.

COMFORT FIRE

Camping Cookbook

What if you could bring comfort and warmth to the campfire? Well, with the reflected flame, you can. On cold nights, you just don't need a simple conical tent to keep you warm. You need to focus the heat on you directly. The problem with most campfires is that they emit heat in all directions. Inverter Fire Barrier solves this problem by repeating the way the burner works. The background of the fireplace reflects the heat to the home. The inverter does exactly the same.

You can use any type of fire to make reflectors, tents, cabins, sparks, etc. We put the fire in front of the background just to reflect the heat.

Try to find a natural reflector to ignite the ignition source in front of it. Slopes, large rocks, or earthen dams will work. If you do not find a natural reflector, you can push two full wooden quantities from the fire's front to the ground at an angle to build your reflector. Relying on these inclined bars, a row of records from the largest to the smallest is stacked to form a stop station as a reflector. Use the only greenwood to avoid burning.

ALTERNATIVE HEAT SOURCES

Before settling in, explore any potential campsite for possible hazards, such as poison ivy, rockslides, or dangerous currents. Remind your fellow campers (especially children) of sensible safety rules such as never swimming alone.

Since you know you need fire, you will need a combustion device as an element of your kit. There are numerous primitive ways to start a fire—so many that I could write a second volume to cover them—but remember, you are "smoothing it." You can practice your skills and "craft," but you need to be prepared as well. Fire is very difficult to create from only natural materials, especially in some environments, and it requires a high level of skill. There are three reliable methods of ignition readily available today:

Lighters

As with any other piece of gear, there are thousands of varieties of lighters available to you. Which is the best? The most reliable in adverse weather conditions, it lasts the longest in your backpack when not in use and has to be easy to use when needed. The regular BIC brand lighter is the forerunner in this category. Lighters that require adding fluid fuels are prone to evaporation, and if they need parts replaced and are not a throwaway item, they are too complicated to be reliable. For ease of use, it is

Camping Cookbook

hard to beat flicking the BIC! Don't settle for the cheap imitations; get a real BIC, and if possible, get it in orange so you can readily find it.

You should have at least three lighters: one for the pocket, one for the belt pouch or haversack, and one for the main pack. The weight is negligible, and the reward is great. The rule of thumb for a lighter or other open-flame device is five seconds to ignite the tinder; any further use is wasting a resource.

Ferrocerium Rods

Ferrocerium rods, metal match, mischmetal—these are all synonymous terms. A ferrocerium rod is a solid rod made from pyrophoric materials, such as iron, magnesium, cerium, lanthanum, neodymium, and praseodymium. Some of these materials have a very low combustion temperature, and when you create friction against the rod, combustion occurs. To accomplish this, you need a 90° sharp edge that is harder than the rod's material. This harder edge will remove the material and create a spark that is approximately 3,000°F. For use in the woods, it is best to have the largest and longest rod possible, increasing the surface area and friction over distance. A longer rod will have more material removed when you strike it, and it will create more burning metal (sparks). I prefer to carry a blank rod that is 1/2" in diameter and 6" long, with the end wrapped in 1" duct tape. (This creates a handle and acts as an emergency flame extender as well.) Many rods have handles of plastic, wood, or even antlers, but unless they are actually drilled and pinned, there is no epoxy to keep the rod from eventually coming out of the handle.

Magnification Lens (Sun Glass)

From the point of view of resource management for your kit, the magnifying glass or "sun lens" is really the best fire-starting method. If the sun is shining, you need only natural materials to make an ember. If you have made charred material, this will be easily ignited in seconds by the sun. Any lens carried should be at least 5x magnifications; size is actually more critical than magnification's power. The larger the surface area to collect the sun's rays, the better it will work. You do not need to go overboard in this aspect. However, a simple lens that is 1 1/2–2" in diameter will work fine.

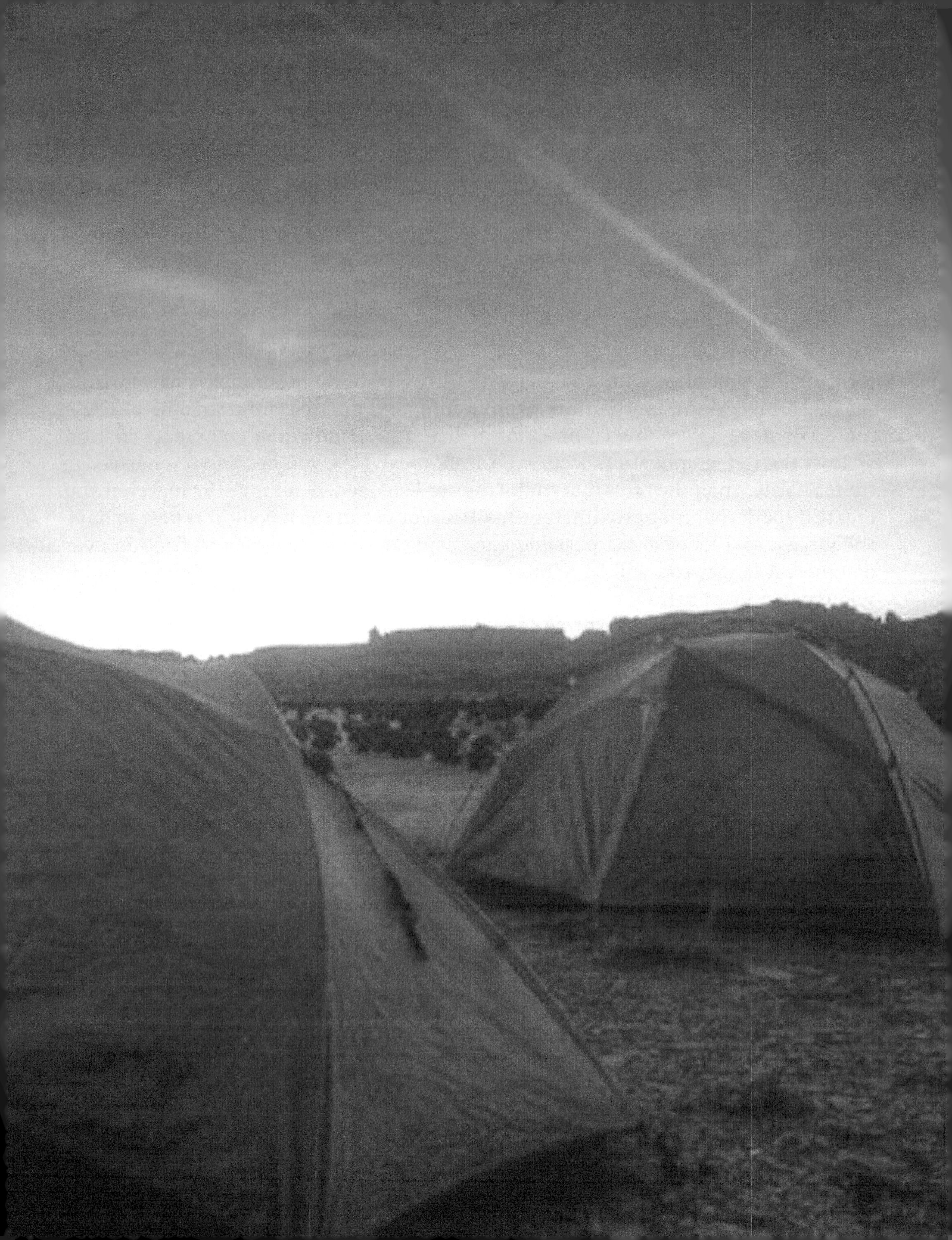

Chapter 4 Do's and Don'ts

Much of the cooking within this book refers to the open-flame style of cooking.

Fire safety is essential. Always keep an eye on the fire, never leave it unattended, and make sure that the fire is completely out, even if it is in a fire ring. Keep fire extinguishers at the ready, just in case.

Second, fire cooking is a tricky business. Until you know how to judge the heat of a fire or its coals, you may first face some challenges. The best way to attain success is to keep vigilant while cooking. Note that the best way to cook is directly on hot coals. This means you must have the time to start a fire, make it hot, and then let it die down into coals. If you do not have this time or patience, you might want to consider alternatives, as cooking over a flame though good, is trickier. Using a grill is helpful, and moving the food consistently may help prevent scorching. If you do not feel comfortable cooking over an open flame, any camp stove will work quite well.

Do not forget to put the fire out after you are finished using it. One of the best ways to do this is to cover it with sand or dirt until it dies off completely.

Here are some additional tips regarding food safety. While this list is by no means exhaustive, it is a good starting point.

- Washing your hands before and after handling food is an important safety rule to follow at all times. It may be even more so when cooking outside. You can also use hand sanitizers.

- Working on a clean surface and keeping bugs and undesired creepy crawlers out of your food supply is also vital to avoid food poisoning. If you can, keeping your cooler in your car or trailer is a really good way to avoid contamination.

- Wash your fruits and vegetables with safe, drinkable water.

Camping Cookbook

- Drink a bottle you've bought or brought from home to make sure the water supply you use is safe to drink.

- Clean-up immediately after each meal, storing leftover food in airtight containers and away from night prowlers.

FOOD SECURITY

All that said, special care should be taken when preparing your foods on site. Many of these recipes include foods that require refrigeration. Keep all foods in a cooler filled with ice or in a refrigerator until cooking. This is especially true for raw meats, dairy, and eggs. When preparing raw meats (and eggs), be careful not to cross-contaminate. This is when raw meat juices spread to other foods, like vegetables, which may be left raw. This is a problem because botulism and other bacteria can cause serious illness when consumed, even in small quantities. Make sure to wash hands, knives, and prep materials between each dish. Keeping a cutting board and knives for each food item (green for vegetables, white for meat, for example) can help prevent cross-contamination. You may wish to prepare as much as possible before your camping trip.

SAFETY TIPS CLEAN-UP TIPS

1. Before sparking the fire, clear all fire areas of twigs, leaves, and brush.

2. Leave no trace before exiting the campsite and gather all garbage or waste. Leave things better than you discovered them.

3. Ensure that there are no trenches and gaps underneath your tent; otherwise, you will get washed out if it rains.

4. Place garbage and food in a heavy container or clip it into a tree, or else you're going to have a starving, vicious animal camping spot. DO NOT bring food in your shelters, or you're going to end up face to face with a starving raccoon.

5. Making sure it's robust and secure with all your tools.

6. There are definitely no fires in your tent or well, you know what's going to happen.

Camping Cookbook

7. Be prepared for something that might arise, have the appropriate supplies. Before you go, check the weather.

8. Keep away from tall trees or something metal; there may be a severe lightning storm. Put your tent down.

9. If a storm occurs, if it is close, get into a ditch or a cellar.

Chapter 5. Type of Cooking Pie Iron

FOIL POCKETS HOBO STYLE

If you're looking for quick and easy camping recipes, foil packet meals are the way to go. All you have to do with most recipes is place the ingredients onto a foil piece, wrap them up and either toss the packet in the campfire or place it on the grill to cook.

Foil packet meals are campfire cooking broken down to the bare essentials. You can whip up entire meals in a few minutes and have dinner done in less than half an hour. Some of the meals in this book are so easy you'll have dinner done in less than 15 minutes.

If you want to save even more time, you can prepare the foil packets ahead of time. All you'll have to do when you get back to your campsite after a long day of camping is grab a handful of foil packets and toss them in the campfire. How's that for an easy meal when all you want to do is relax by the fire?

COOKING TECHNIQUES

There are a number of ways you can cook your foil packets. Here are the most common foil packet cooking methods:

- **In the campfire.** The packets can be placed directly in the campfire. This will cook the food quickly, but it may cook unevenly, as there will be hotspots in the coals.

- **On a grill over the campfire.** A grill over the campfire allows you to utilize your campfire without having to place the foil packets directly in the coals. The food will cook more evenly than it will when the packets are placed in the coals. Don't cook your packets over an open flame. Instead, cook them over hot embers.

- **On a barbecue grill.** Fire up the briquettes and let them burn down to coals. Place the foil packets on the grill to cook. This technique of cooking your foil packet meals gives you the most control over temperature.

Camping Cookbook

- ***In the oven.*** This isn't a camping technique, but you can fire up the oven and cook foil packets when you're at home when you want a quick and easy meal.

Regardless of the cooking direction used, it's important to realize campfire cooking isn't an exact science. The cook times in the recipes in this book are estimates, and many variables can cause them to be wildly inaccurate.

It's important that you monitor your food closely. Check packets regularly while cooking to see how cooked the food inside is. It's best to err on the side of caution when checking packets. If you open a packet and it isn't done yet, you can always put it back on the grill. If you wait too long and the food is burnt, there isn't much you can do to rescue it.

FOIL PACKET COOKING TIPS

Don't worry about being exact. Foil packet recipes are rather forgiving when it comes to the ingredients. I very rarely measure the ingredients I'm putting in a packet. Instead, I throw in a bit of this and a bit of that until I feel like I've got things the way I want them.

Double wrap your foil packets. You don't want to lose half of your food through a hole in the bottom of your packet. You also don't want to accidentally poke a hole in your packet while eating and have hot juices run out into your lap.

If you're planning on dumping the foil packet contents onto a plate to eat them, cut the top off of the foil packet with a pair of scissors. The foil packet will be hot and trying to unfold; it is an exercise in frustration. Using scissors will allow you to open the packet without burning your fingers.

Use boiled vegetables to speed things up. Pre-cooked carrots, potatoes and celery will really speed up the cooking times for recipes that call for these items.

When you're cooking foods that don't have a lot of moisture, add a bit of butter to the foil packet inside to keep the food from sticking to the foil. ***Cooking spray will also work.***

You can eat your food straight out of the foil packet if you want. Cut an X in the top of the foil packet and fold the foil back, giving you easy access to your food.

You can speed things up in a couple of ways. Create the spice blends ahead of time and bring them in a Ziploc baggy. Another way to speed things up is to create the foil packets in advance and bring the ready-to-go packets in the ice chest. All you'll have to do is toss the packets on the fire.

Chapter 6. Car Camping

CAR CAMPING ESSENTIALS

- Tent
- Sleeping bags
- Headlamps or flashlights
- Camp chairs
- Lantern
- Extra cord
- Firestarter/matches
- Cook pots
- Potholder
- Dutch oven
- Eating utensils
- Sharp knife
- Bottle opener/can opener/corkscrew
- Cups
- Camp grill
- Grill rack/grate
- Charcoal
- Portable tea/coffee maker
- Sunscreen
- Insect repellent
- First-aid kit

Camping Cookbook

Chapter 7. Breakfast

Camping Cookbook

WILD BERRY BREAKFAST BREAD PUDDING

Beginner | 30 minutes | Breakfast | 04 Servings

INGREDIENTS

- 4 cups of cubed French or cinnamon bread
- ½ cup of strawberries, quartered
- ½ cup of blackberries, halved
- ½ cup of blueberries
- 2 eggs, beaten
- 1 cup of cream or whole milk
- ½ cup of brown sugar
- 1 teaspoon of cinnamon
- ½ teaspoon of nutmeg
- 1 teaspoon of orange extract
- 18"x18" or larger piece of greased aluminum foil

COOKING STEPS

1. Packet folding style: tent
2. In a bag or bowl, combine the eggs, cream, brown sugar, cinnamon, nutmeg, and orange extract. Add the cubed bread and saturate for at least 15 minutes.
3. Add the berry mixture to the bag and blend. Transfer the contents to the center of a large, greased piece of foil.
4. Create a tent style fold and place the packet onto the heat source.
5. Cook for 30-35 minutes or until the bread pudding is cooked through. Make sure it still maintains moisture.

Nutrition:

Calories: 224   Fat: 12   Fiber: 5   Carbs: 15   Protein: 5

ORANGE CHOCO-NUT ENERGY MUFFINS

Beginner   40 minutes   Breakfast   4 Servings

INGREDIENTS

- 1½ cups of all-purpose flour
- ¼ cup of white sugar
- ¼ cup of brown sugar
- ½ cup of dark chocolate chips
- ¼ cup of shredded coconut
- ¼ cup of chopped walnuts
- ¼ teaspoon of salt
- ½ teaspoon of cinnamon
- ½ cup of milk
- ¼ cup of vegetable oil
- 1 tablespoon of fresh-squeezed orange juice
- 8 oranges, cut in half with insides removed
- 8 6"x6" pieces of greased aluminum foil

1. Packet folding style: tight wrap
2. In a large bowl, combine all of the dry ingredients, including the flour, white sugar, brown sugar, chocolate chips, coconut, walnuts, salt and cinnamon. Set aside.
3. Take the oranges and cut each in half width-wise, reserving any juice. Scoop out the pulp to create hollow shells.
4. Add the milk, vegetable oil, and orange juice to the dry ingredients.
5. Fill one-half of each orange shell with the muffin mixture. Top with the other half of the orange shell. Wrap each orange tightly in a greased sheet of aluminum foil.
6. Place oranges onto the heat source and cook for 15-20 minutes, turning occasionally.
7. Remove from heat and let cool 10 minutes before opening.

Nutrition:

Calories: 183   Fat: 12   Fiber: 5   Carbs: 15   Protein: 4

JERK CHICKEN LEGS

Easy | 50 minutes | Breakfast | 4 Servings

INGREDIENTS

- 4 chicken legs with thighs
- 1 Habanero chili pepper, trimmed and sliced
- 1 onion
- 1 scallion
- 2 garlic cloves
- ⅓ cup of soy sauce
- 1 teaspoon of 5 spice powder
- ¼ teaspoon of nutmeg
- ¼ teaspoon of cinnamon
- 1 teaspoon of salt

COOKING STEPS

1. You'll need to make this marinade ahead of time since you need to use a blender.

2. Mix the chicken in a blender, and mix until fairly smooth.

3. Place the marinade and the chicken legs in a freezer bag, and marinate the night before you leave for your trip up to 12 hours.

4. Heat grill to medium-high, coat with vegetable oil, cook the chicken legs for approximately 25 minutes and turn halfway through.

5. Serve with rice or a pasta salad.

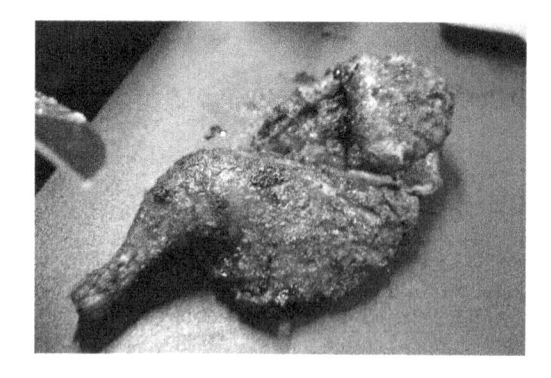

Nutrition:

Calories: 213   Fat: 12   Fiber: 2   Carbs: 5   Protein: 15

BEER CHICKEN AND FINGERLING POTATOES

Beginner   40 minutes   Breakfast   4 Servings

INGREDIENTS

- 8 chicken thighs
- 1 can of dark beer
- ½ cup of BBQ sauce
- 20 fingerling potatoes
- 1 teaspoon of rosemary
- 1 teaspoon of salt
- 1 teaspoon of black pepper
- Vegetable oil

COOKING STEPS

6. Combine the beer, BBQ sauce, ½ teaspoon of salt, ½ teaspoon of black pepper, ½ teaspoon of paprika in the dish, add chicken thighs, and marinate for an hour.
7. Combine 3 tablespoons of vegetable oil with a teaspoon of rosemary and ½ teaspoon of salt, and mix.
8. Slice potatoes in half, and add to the oil mixture, set aside.
9. Light your fire, and wait until flames die down and hot coals remain.
10. Coat grate with vegetable oil.
11. Place chicken and potatoes on the grate.

Nutrition:

Calories: 275   Fat: 27   Fiber: 3   Carbs: 15   Protein: 25

Camping Cookbook

ORANGE GINGER WINGS

Beginner   40 minutes   Breakfast   04 Servings

INGREDIENTS

- 2 pounds of chicken wings
- 1 tablespoon of ginger, grated
- ½ cup of soy sauce
- ¼ cup of honey
- ¼ cup of orange juice
- ½ teaspoon of red pepper
- ½ teaspoon of black pepper

COOKING STEPS

1. Combine ginger, ¼ cup of soy, orange juice, black pepper, and red pepper in a bowl.
2. Marinate the chicken wings in orange-ginger sauce for an hour.
3. Fire up the grill, and cook the chicken wings for 20 minutes, turning twice through the process.
4. Mix honey with remaining soy sauce, and drizzle over wings.
5. Serve with celery and carrot sticks or your choice of side.

Nutrition:

Calories: 312   Fat: 17   Fiber: 3   Carbs: 10   Protein: 45

FLINTSTONE STEAK AND LEMONY ASPARAGUS

Beginner   25 minutes   Breakfast   4 Servings

INGREDIENTS

- 2 bone-in 1.5" rib-eye steaks
- 1 pound of asparagus, tough ends removed
- 4 tablespoons of extra virgin olive oil
- 1 lemon, juiced
- Salt
- Black pepper
- Vegetable oil

COOKING STEPS

1. Generously season rib steaks with salt and black pepper, and let them rest for 20 minutes.
2. Mix extra virgin olive oil, lemon juice, 1 teaspoon of salt, and drizzle on asparagus.
3. Make sure your fire is medium-high and using a rag, generously coat your grate with oil.
4. Place steaks on the grate, and cook for 4 minutes per side for medium-rare.
5. Place asparagus on the grill, and cook for 5 minutes, turning ⅓ of the way after a minute, turning ⅓ of the way again after 2 minutes, and again after another minute.
6. Slice up your steak and serve with asparagus.

Nutrition:

Calories: 293   Fat: 12   Fiber: 7   Carbs: 15   Protein: 32

RECIPE TITLE 1

Simple One-line Description about the Titled Recipe

Intermediate | 50 minutes | Breakfast | 4 Servings

INGREDIENTS

- 4 beef loin steaks
- 3 tablespoons of mustard
- 4 pickles, speared
- 4 slices of black forest ham
- 1 onion, chopped
- Salt
- Black pepper

COOKING STEPS

1. Pound the beefsteak, so it is approximately ¼" thin. Sprinkle generously with salt and black pepper; let it rest for 20 minutes.
2. Slice black forest ham into bite-sized pieces, and combine with the onion.
3. Spread mustard over one side of the steak, spoon ham, and onion mixture onto mustard. Add pickle spear.
4. Roll roulade over your roasting stick and secure with butcher's twine.
5. Roast for 7 minutes over an open fire.

Nutrition:

Calories: 234   Fat: 9   Fiber: 7   Carbs: 28   Protein: 34

Camping Cookbook

CHARRED PEACHES

Intermediate | 20 minutes | Breakfast | 4 Servings

INGREDIENTS

- 4 peaches, halved, pitted and skin removed
- 1 teaspoon of cinnamon
- 1 tablespoon of brown sugar
- Vegetable oil
- Whipped cream topping, optional

COOKING STEPS

1. Sprinkle peaches halves with cinnamon.
2. Place grate over indirect heat and brush grate with vegetable oil.
3. Grill peaches face down for 2-3 minutes until heated through and lightly charred.
4. Flip over and sprinkle with brown sugar. Grill for 1 to 2 minutes more or until brown sugar is melted (starting to caramelize) and peaches are tender.
5. Serve with the whipped cream topping, if desired.

Nutrition:

Calories: 189 | Fat: 10 | Fiber: 10 | Carbs: 35 | Protein: 5

Camping Cookbook

EGG IN AN AVOCADO

| Intermediate | 30 minutes | Breakfast | 4 Servings |

INGREDIENTS

- 1 half avocado
- 1 egg
- Salt and pepper to taste

COOKING STEPS

1. Cut avocado in half and remove the seed. Scoop out part of the avocado to make room for the egg.
2. Crack the egg and dump the contents into the avocado.
3. Wrap in foil.
4. Cook for 15 to 20 minutes, or until the egg is cooked to your liking.
5. Carefully unwrap the packet and season the egg with salt and pepper.

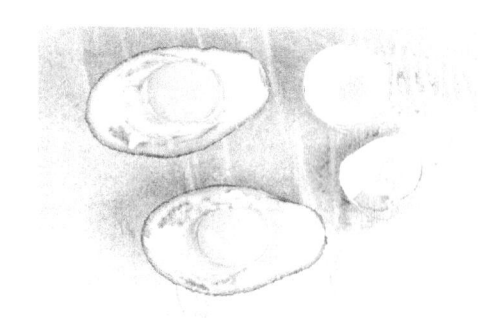

Nutrition:

Calories: 149   Fat: 12   Fiber: 2   Carbs: 10   Protein: 19

Camping Cookbook

EGG MUFFIN

Intermediate | 25 minutes | Breakfast | 4 Servings

INGREDIENTS

- 1 English muffin
- 1 slice cheddar cheese
- 1 hash brown patty
- 1 sausage patty
- 1 egg
- Salt and pepper, to taste

COOKING STEPS

1. Place the hash brown patty on the foil.
2. Wrap the packet around the hash brown patty. Leave the top open.
3. Crack the egg and dump the contents over the top of the hash brown patty.
4. Place the sausage patty on top of the egg.
5. Close the foil packet.
6. Cook for 10 to 15 minutes, or until the egg is cooked to your liking.
7. Remove packet from heat.
8. Open packet and season with salt and pepper.
9. Place the contents of the packet in half like an English muffin. Add cheese to the top and place the other half of the muffin on top to make a sandwich.

Nutrition:

Calories: 148   Fat: 12   Fiber: 2   Carbs: 13   Protein: 24

ORANGE PEEL EGGS

Intermediate | 25 minutes | Breakfast | 4 Servings

INGREDIENTS

- ✓ 1 orange
- ✓ 2 eggs
- ✓ Salt and pepper, to taste

COOKING STEPS

1. Cut the orange in half and scoop out the meat. Leave the peel intact. When done, you should have 2 empty orange halves.
2. Crack an egg into each of the orange halves.
3. Wrap each half in its own foil packet. Be careful to keep the orange peel upright, so the egg doesn't spill out.
4. Cook the packet for 10 to 15 minutes, or until the eggs are cooked all the way through.
5. Remove the packet from the heat.
6. Open it carefully and season the egg with salt and pepper.

Nutrition:

Calories: 179 | Fat: 10 | Fiber: 7 | Carbs: 15 | Protein: 17

Camping Cookbook

SAUSAGE, PEPPERS AND ZUCCHINI

Camp Master | 40 minutes | Breakfast | 4 Servings

INGREDIENTS

- 1 large sausage, sliced diagonally
- 1 zucchini, sliced diagonally
- 5 new potatoes, quartered
- 1 red bell pepper, seeded and sliced
- ½ medium onion, sliced
- Salt and pepper, to taste

COOKING STEPS

1. Combine all the ingredients in a foil packet.
2. Seal the packet up tightly.
3. Cook for 25 to 30 minutes, or until sausage is cooked and vegetables are soft.

Nutrition:

Calories: 338   Fat: 18   Fiber: 10   Carbs: 37   Protein: 29

Camping Cookbook

STEAK AND EGGS

Camp Master | 35 minutes | Breakfast | 4 Servings

INGREDIENTS

- ½ pound of roast meat
- 2 tablespoons of taco seasoning
- 2 eggs
- ½ cup of Mexican blend cheese

COOKING STEPS

1. Cut the roast meat up and place it in a foil packet with taco seasoning.
2. Crack the eggs and dump them into the packet.
3. Mix the steak and eggs together.
4. Cook for 15 to 20 minutes or until steak and eggs are cooked.
5. Open foil packet and sprinkle cheese on top.
6. Eat the steak and eggs on their own or add them to a tortilla to make a breakfast burrito.

Nutrition:

Calories: 378   Fat: 18   Fiber: 7   Carbs: 14   Protein: 47

Camping Cookbook

LOGS AND EGGS EASY BREAKFAST PACKET

Camp Master   40 minutes   Breakfast   4 Servings

INGREDIENTS

- 12 sausage links
- 8 eggs
- 2 cups of prepared hash browns
- ½ cup of onion, diced
- ¼ cup of green pepper, diced
- 1 cup of cheddar cheese, shredded
- ½ teaspoon of garlic powder
- ½ teaspoon of salt
- ½ teaspoon of black pepper
- 4 8"x8" or larger pieces of greased aluminum foil

COOKING STEPS

1. Packet folding style: Tent
2. Place three sausage links in the middle of each piece of aluminum foil.
3. Top the sausage links with the hash browns, the onions, peppers, and finally the cheese.
4. Season to taste with garlic powder, salt, and pepper.
5. Tent fold the packet and place onto the heat source, turning occasionally, for 20 minutes or until the sausage's internal temperature reaches 165°F.

Nutrition:

Calories: 218   Fat: 19   Fiber: 3   Carbs: 15   Protein: 39

Camping Cookbook

GREEN CHILE BREAKFAST BURRITOS

Camp Master · 25 minutes · Breakfast · 4 Servings

INGREDIENTS

- 4 large flour tortillas
- 2 cups of spicy ground sausage, precooked
- 1 cup of canned refried beans
- 4 eggs, beaten
- 1 cup of Monterey Jack cheese, shredded
- 1 cup of prepared Salsa Verde
- 4 12x12 pieces of greased aluminum foil

COOKING STEPS

1. Packet folding style: Flat
2. Place one flour tortilla in the center of each piece of aluminum foil.
3. Top the tortillas with a layer of refried beans, then with the sausage and eggs. You may want to fold up the tortillas' ends as you pour in the eggs to reduce spillage.
4. Finally, add the cheese and Salsa Verde to taste.
5. Roll each tortilla tightly, making sure to seal the ends and create a flat style fold with the aluminum foil.
6. Place packets on the heat source, turning every few minutes for ten minutes, or to taste.

Nutrition:

Calories: 239   Fat: 12   Fiber: 6   Carbs: 19   Protein: 35

BACON AND POTATO HASH

Camp Master | 30 minutes | Breakfast | 4 Servings

INGREDIENTS

- 4 cups of hash brown potatoes
- ½ pound of bacon, diced and cooked
- 1 cup of yellow onion, diced
- 1 cup of corn kernels
- 1 cup of Colby cheese, shredded
- 1 teaspoon of Cajun seasoning
- 1 teaspoon of salt
- 1 teaspoon of black pepper
- 4 8"x8" or larger pieces of greased aluminum foil

COOKING STEPS

1. Packet folding style: Tent
2. Season the hash browns with Cajun seasoning, salt, and pepper.
3. Place 1 cup of potatoes onto the center of each piece of foil
4. Add the bacon, onion, corn, and cheese.
5. Produce a tent style fold and place the packets onto the heat source, occasionally turning, for 15 minutes or until ingredients are heated throughout. Leave on a few minutes longer for crispier potatoes.

Nutrition:

Calories: 387   Fat: 13   Fiber: 7   Carbs: 12   Protein: 28

VEGETARIAN BREAKFAST CROISSANT SANDWICHES

Camp Master | 25 minutes | Breakfast | 4 Servings

INGREDIENTS

- 4 bakery croissants split in half
- 1 medium tomato, sliced
- 1 cup of fresh spinach
- 1 avocado, peeled and sliced into eight wedges
- 2 tablespoons of walnuts, chopped
- 4 slices provolone cheese, optional
- 1 teaspoon of Italian seasoning
- ½ teaspoon of black pepper
- 4 12"x12" pieces of greased aluminum foil

COOKING STEPS

1. Packet folding style: Flat
2. Take each of the four croissants and lay one-half of each in the center of an aluminium foil piece.
3. Stack the ingredients onto the croissant, starting with the spinach, then the tomatoes, avocados, walnuts, and cheese.
4. Season with Italian seasoning and black pepper before applying to the top of the croissant.
5. Create a tight, flat fold over each croissant and place on the heat source for 5-10 minutes or until the sandwich is hot and steamy.

Nutrition:

Calories: 278   Fat: 7   Fiber: 5   Carbs: 32   Protein: 7

Chapter 8. Lunch and Dinner

Camping Cookbook

SERVE BLUEBERRY PORK BELLY WITH ROAST CORN AND A GREEN SALAD

Beginner | 70 minutes | Lunch and Dinner | 4 Servings

INGREDIENTS

- 1 pound of pork belly
- 1 cup of blueberries
- ½ cup of sherry
- 1 chicken bouillon cube

COOKING STEPS

1. Mashup the blueberries with sherry and mix in a bouillon cube and set aside.

2. Heat your grill to medium-high, push aside coals from one section. This is where you will cook your pork belly.

3. Brush your pork belly with the blueberry mixture, and place on grill, cook for 2 hours while basting every 20 minutes.

Nutrition:

Calories: 387   Fat: 9   Fiber: 13   Carbs: 39   Protein: 28

Camping Cookbook

BACON AND SWEET POTATO SKEWERS

Beginner | 25 minutes | Lunch and Dinner | 4/6 Servings

INGREDIENTS

- ✓ 2 sweet potatoes
- ✓ 8 bacon slices
- ✓ 1 teaspoon of oregano
- ✓ 1 teaspoon of salt
- ✓ 3 tablespoons of extra virgin olive oil

COOKING STEPS

1. Combine olive oil with salt and oregano.
2. Slice sweet potatoes into 1" cubes.
3. Skewer sweet potatoes, and brush with olive oil mixture.
4. Wrap skewers with bacon.
5. Heat grill to medium, place skewers over indirect heat, and grill for 12 minutes or until potatoes are juicy and tender.
6. You can serve these skewers with eggs at breakfast or with a big salad for lunch or dinner.

Nutrition:

Calories: 276   Fat: 18   Fiber: 7   Carbs: 13   Protein: 26

Camping Cookbook

LAMB AND ZUCCHINI SHISH

Beginner | 20 minutes | Lunch and Dinner | 4 Servings

INGREDIENTS

- 2 pounds of boneless leg of lamb, trimmed
- 3 zucchinis
- 4 garlic cloves, chopped
- 1 teaspoon of rosemary
- 1 teaspoon of oregano
- 1 teaspoon of salt
- 1 teaspoon of black peppery
- Extra virgin olive oil
- Pita bread

COOKING STEPS

1. Prepare garlic paste ahead of time if using a blender, if taking along a mortar and pestle you can do it at the campsite.
2. Combine garlic cloves, rosemary, oregano, salt, black pepper, and ¼-cup of olive oil, blend or pound into a paste.
3. Slice leg of lamb into 1" cubes and coat with garlic paste, allow to marinate for an hour.
4. Slice zucchini into 1" cubes.
5. Thread zucchini and lamb amongst 8 skewers.
6. Fire up your grill to medium-high and cook skewers for approximately 7 minutes for medium-rare.
7. You can serve your skewers with pita bread.

Nutrition:

Calories: 398   Fat: 14   Fiber: 8   Carbs: 23   Protein: 19

GARLIC-INFUSED LEG OF LAMB

Beginner | 130 minutes | Lunch and Dinner | 12/16 Servings

INGREDIENTS

- 1 boneless leg of lamb, about 8 pounds
- 8 garlic cloves, chopped
- 1 tablespoon of rosemary
- 2 tablespoons of oregano
- 2 tablespoons of salt
- 1 teaspoon of black peppery
- ¼ cup of extra virgin olive oil

COOKING STEPS

1. You will need to have your fire area set up for the stick-spit method.
2. Prepare garlic paste ahead of time if using a blender. If taking along a mortar and pestle, you can do it at the campsite.
3. Combine garlic cloves, rosemary, oregano, salt, black pepper and ¼ cup of olive oil, blend or pound into a paste.
4. Rub lamb with paste, secure on spit stick.
5. Place lamb at least 5" above medium-high heat and cook for about 20 minutes while turning every 7 minutes.
6. You can move the lamb over indirect heat and cook for 2 hours or until the internal temperature is 130°F.
7. Serve with potatoes and veggies to your liking.

Nutrition:

Calories: 336 | Fat: 16 | Fiber: 7 | Carbs: 19 | Protein: 39

CAMPFIRE SKILLET CORNBREAD

Beginner | 30 minutes | Lunch and Dinner | 8 Servings

INGREDIENTS

- 1 tbsp. of Baking powder
- ½ cup of Flour
- 1 cup of Med grind cornmeal
- 1/2 tbsp. of Oil
- 1 Egg
- 1 cup of Milk
- ½ tbsp. of Salt
- 2 tbsp. of Honey

COOKING STEPS

1. Combine the flour, cornmeal, salt & baking powder in a wide bowl.

2. In dry ingredients, add the egg, honey & milk. Mix it until completely combined.

3. Heat the oil in the iron frying pan over the fire, cover the bottom and turn it over. Place the batter in the pan, making sure all is in the even layer. Cover the pan with foil crimping a foil across the corners.

4. Cook for 15 min on med-low heat, then step away from the heat and allow the bread to rest for an extra five min (also now covered). Cut it into slices and enjoy it.

Nutrition:

Calories: 288   Fat: 14   Fiber: 11   Carbs: 27   Protein: 11

Camping Cookbook

DRUNKEN CAULIFLOWER TACOS WITH QUICK PICKLED RED ONIONS

Beginner | 25 minutes | Lunch and Dinner | 6 Servings

INGREDIENTS

- Cauliflower Tacos
- 2 tbsp. of Cumin
- 1 head Chopped cauliflower
- 2 tbsp. of Dried oregano
- 1/8 tbsp. of Cayenne
- 1 tbsp. of Sea salt
- 6 Corn tortillas
- 2 cloves of minced garlic
- 1 tbsp. of Olive oil
- ½ cup of Lager beer
- Quick pickled onions
- 2/3 Juiced limes
- 1 small Sliced red onions

COOKING STEPS

1. Prepare the fast-pickled onions: in a tiny bowl, add the lime juice, salt, and onions. Have them stay for around 15 to 20 min, tossing per 5 min.

2. Cook the cauliflower: put cumin, beer, salt, dried oregano, garlic, and cayenne to the cauliflower in a pan. Carry to a boil fast. Boil until all the liquid has vaporized, stirring regularly. If the liquid has vaporized, put the olive oil and fry until the cauliflower is soft and brown at the beginning.

3. Heat the tortillas: Heat the tortillas when the cauliflower is frying. We do this for 1 tortilla in the stove burner, rotating every 15-20 sec so that all sides are toasty. This may be completed on a campfire as well, or in the oven, if you're at home.

4. Assemble the tacos: fill every tortilla with the scoop of pickled red onions, cauliflower, and some extra toppings

Nutrition:

Calories 301 | Fat 13 | Fiber 4 | Carbs 29 | Protein 18

SWEET & SAVORY GRILLED TEMPEH

Beginner | 30 minutes | Lunch and Dinner | 4 Servings

INGREDIENTS

- 8 oz. of Tempeh
- 2 tbsp. of Soy sauce
- 1/4 cup of Maple syrup

COOKING STEPS

1. In a zip-lock plastic bag wide enough to carry the tempeh, mix the soya sauce, apple cider vinegar, and maple syrup.

2. Slice your tempeh into four slices. With marinade, put them within a zip lock bag. Be sure that the slices of tempeh are equally coated & allow for at least thirty min to marinate.

3. Grill/barbecue the tempeh on the campfire or roast it with a hint of oil in the cast iron pan. Cook on both sides for 2 to 3 min.

Nutrition:

Calories 181   Fat 4   Fiber 3   Carbs 13   Protein 6

Camping Cookbook

ARTICHOKE & POBLANO CAMPFIRE PAELLA

Beginner | 40 minutes | Lunch and Dinner | 2 Servings

INGREDIENTS

- 2 Poblano peppers
- 1 large Diced shallot
- 3 Green onions
- 3 cloves Roughly minced garlic
- ¼ cup of Tempranillo
- 14 oz. of can Broth
- 14 oz. of can Halved & drained artichoke hearts
- ½ cup of Rice
- Saffron pinch
- ½ tbsp. of Salt
- 2 tbsp. of Olive

COOKING STEPS

1. Put the green onions, sausage and Poblano peppers directly on the fire on the grill pan, rotating periodically, until the onions and peppers are tender, crispy and the sausage is cooked completely.

2. Take it from your grill. Cut your sausage into pieces of around 1/4 inch. Let the peppers chill, extract the seeds, peel the skin off, and chop. Mince the green onions into bite-sized bits.

3. Put the cast iron pan straight on over fire on the barbecue/grill. To cover the bottom of the pan, add plenty of oil and then place the shallots. Sauté for 3 to 5 minutes until it is smooth.

4. Place the garlic sliced, sausage and sauté for around 30 sec, until the garlic is aromatic.

5. Put the rice and cook for 2 to 3 min, often mixing until the ends are only translucent.

6. Place 1/4 cup red wine in the skillet and allow vaporizing. After that, put the broth. Add salt as well as a pinch of saffron to season. Mix

Camping Cookbook

   well to spread all the ingredients equally, and then leave 20 to 30 minutes to boil, undisturbed, until all the liquid has been absorbed.

7. To reheat, add to the skillet the sliced green onions, artichoke hearts, and Poblano. At that moment, the paella on the bottom will start forming the Socarrat. You would start hearing the rice beginning to crackle within a few minutes that's the sign here that the dish is almost finished. To ensure that the Socarrat has formed, cook for another few minutes.

8. Serve immediately.

Nutrition:

Calories: 278   Fat: 9   Fiber: 9   Carbs: 29   Protein: 18

Camping Cookbook

SHAKSHUKA

Beginner | 25 minutes | Lunch and Dinner | 4 Servings

INGREDIENTS

- 1 Seeded and sliced red bell pepper
- 1 Diced small onion
- 3 cloves of Chopped garlic
- 2 tbsp. of Paprika
- Minced parsley
- 1/4 cup of Feta cheese
- 14 oz. of can Diced tomatoes
- 1 tbsp. of Cumin
- 1 Sliced & seeded Poblano peppers
- Pepper & salt
- 1 tbsp. of Olive oil

COOKING STEPS

1. Warm oil over low heat in your pan. When the Poblano, red bell peppers and onions are warmed, swirl to cover, and cook for five minutes or until the color changes to brown, stirring if required. Put the paprika, cumin and garlic then cook for around thirty sec until it is fragrant.

2. Place the tomatoes as well as their juices. To allow the combination to thicken, lower the heat and boil for 10 min.

3. Break the eggs into the sauce, uniformly spaced them apart. Cover and let the eggs boil until the whites are set, 5 to 7 minutes to allow them to cook completely, you may spoon that sauce on over top as required.

4. Top to taste. Serve with feta cheese, sliced parsley, and a couple of pieces of crusty bread.

Nutrition:

Calories: 276 | Fat: 14 | Fiber: 3 | Carbs: 19 | Protein: 29

CAMPFIRE PIZZA MARGHERITA

Beginner | 40 minutes | Lunch and Dinner | 2 Servings

INGREDIENTS

For the crust:
- 1 packet rapid rise yeast
- 1 cup of warm water
- 5 tbsp. of Olive oil
- 2 ½ cups of Flour
- 2 tbsp. of Salt

Toppings:
- 1 large tomato sliced into 1/4-inch
- 8 oz. of mozzarella balls cut into 1/4-inch rounds
- 2 tbsp. Cut into ribbons fresh basil
- 1/2 cup of Tomato sauce

COOKING STEPS

1. Add the yeast, salt and flour into a food processor or bowl. To split the ingredients, gently combine them with a fork.

2. To dry ingredients, add the hot water and 2 tbsp. of oil and combine with the fork until the ingredients start to shape the dough.

3. Knead your dough a couple of times so all the components are very well combined and the dough stays together.

4. Cover your dough for twenty minutes and allow it to rise.

5. Turn it out on a chopping board once your dough has risen, then split the dough into 2 separate parts.

6. In a 10-inch cast-iron pan, put 1 tbsp. of oil to make the crust and swirl to cover the top. Put one of the dough halves within the pan, push and press the dough into the pan's sides with the fingers. Sprinkle 1/2 tbsp. of oil with the sides of the pan.

7. Put the pan at suitably high heat on a grate on the campfire/camp stove. Cook for 3 to 5 min, until the bottom has tightened up and

Camping Cookbook

starts to change to a golden brown.

8. Remove the pan from the heat & put it on a heat-safe surface. The pan would be hot, so stay aware of the next few stages.

9. Take a crust out from the pan by using 2 tongs and flip it so that the pan's non-cooked part is face-down.

10. Split the tomato sauce 1/4 cup over on the top of the pizza, after this layer the minced tomatoes and mozzarella. Season the top with basil.

11. Bring the pizza to the stove/campfire. Cook the pizza until the bottom becomes golden brown for 3 to 5 minutes. After some minutes, remove the foil or lid when the cheese is melted to allow the steam to escape for the rest of the cooking period.

12. Remove the pan from the oven, move the pizza safely to a dish and repeat for the second half of the dough.

Nutrition:

Calories: 340   Fat: 9   Fiber: 5   Carbs: 26   Protein: 14

Camping Cookbook

DUTCH OVEN CHICKEN MARBELLA

Beginner | 50 minutes | Lunch and Dinner | 4 Servings

INGREDIENTS

- ✓ 1 cup of Halved & pitted olives
- ✓ 1/4 cup of capers
- ✓ 1/2 cup of dry white wine
- ✓ 1 cup of Chopped prunes
- ✓ 6 cloves Roughly minced garlic
- ✓ 2 tbsp. of Dried oregano
- ✓ 1 tbsp. of Salt
- ✓ 2 Bay leaves
- ✓ 1/4 cup of Red wine vinegar
- ✓ 1 tbsp. of Olive oil
- ✓ 4 tbsp. of Brown sugar
- ✓ 4 Skin-on chicken thighs

COOKING STEPS

1. Marinate the chicken: put the bag in the freezer to marinate all ingredients except the brown sugar & oil. For at least 6 hours, and up to 2 days, put in your icebox.

2. Prepare the campfire: twenty-seven prep coals. If you need to, you could use wood embers, although you'll have to measure the right heat ratio (you're looking for 220 c). When all the coals are fully prepared, knock them into just a plain pile & put them all on top of the Dutch oven. This would produce the higher heat needed for browning.

3. Brown the chicken: in the Dutch oven, heat 1 tbsp. of oil. The oil is ready and hot once the water drops sizzles as it hits the skillet. Take your chicken from marinade, and then brush 1 tbsp. of brown sugar over both thighs skin side. Brown the thighs' skin side at a high temperature until the skin becomes crispy and its color changes to a deep golden brown, around 6-8 minutes Please turn to the other side for two minutes

Camping Cookbook

to brown it.

4. Bake: turn off the Dutch oven heat. Put the marinade in the Dutch oven and cover. Spread 18 coals equally on the lid and put 9 coals in the Dutch oven. Bake for 30 minutes, still the thighs are fully cooked, and with there, juices run clear once stabbed with a knife.

5. Serve and enjoy with a few of a sauce spooned on the top, serve it over couscous, pilaf/rice.

Nutrition:

Calories: 224   Fat: 12   Fiber: 5   Carbs: 15   Protein: 5

Camping Cookbook

INDIAN SPICED BAKED POTATO IN FOIL

Beginner   40 minutes   Lunch and Dinner   6 Servings

INGREDIENTS

- 4 cups of Golden yellow potatoes (sliced)
- 3-4 tbsp. of Olive oil
- ½ tbsp. of Smoked paprika
- ½ tbsp. of Garlic (minced)
- ½ tbsp. of Curry powder
- Salt and pepper to taste
- 4 Eggs

COOKING STEPS

1. Combine potatoes and seasonings.
2. Place potatoes in a packet made of foil.
3. Place foil packets over the campfire and cook for 25 to 30 minutes rotating occasionally.
4. Open the foil and pour the beaten eggs, close it again, and cook for an additional few minutes.
5. Remove from fire and garnish with extra spices or seasonings if needed.

Nutrition:

Calories: 224

Fat: 12

Fiber: 5

Carbs: 15

Protein: 5

Camping Cookbook

COUNTRY POTATOES

Intermediate | 45 minutes | Lunch and Dinner | 4 Servings

INGREDIENTS

- 4 Yellow potatoes (thinly sliced)
- 1 onion (sliced)
- 1 clove of Garlic (chopped)
- 4tbsp. of Butter
- 1tbsp. of Basil
- 1tbsp. of Oregano
- Salt and pepper to taste

COOKING STEPS

1. Start by placing 2 tablespoons of butter on the foil's center, then arranging potatoes, garlic, and onion.
2. Sprinkle potatoes with seasonings and add the remaining 2 tablespoons of butter on top.
3. Carefully close foil by bringing ends of the top layer together and cook over a campfire for 30 to 35 minutes.
4. Serve directly from the foil.

Nutrition:

Calories: 253

Fat: 9

Fiber: 3

Carbs: 27

Protein: 12

Camping Cookbook

SHRIMP STEAK FOIL PACKET

Intermediate | 30 minutes | Lunch and Dinner | 4 Servings

INGREDIENTS

- ½ lb./226g of Sirloin steak (cubed)
- ½ lb. /226g of Shrimp (cleaned, deveined)
- 2 ears of Corn (divided into four pieces)
- 1 Red onion (sliced)
- 1 cup cherry tomatoes
- 1 Lemon (wedged)
- 2 cloves Garlic (sliced)
- 4 tbsp. of Olive oil
- 4 sprigs of Thyme
- Salt and pepper, to taste
- 1 tbsp. of Parsley (chopped)

COOKING STEPS

1. Prepare 4 foil packets where you will evenly distribute steak, shrimp, corn, red onion, tomatoes, lemon wedges, and garlic.
2. Season with thyme, salt, and pepper, drizzle with olive oil.
3. Fold the foil paper and cook over campfire or grate for 6 to 8 minutes per side.
4. Sprinkle with parsley before serving.

Nutrition:

Calories: 299 Fat: 16 Fiber: 7 Carbs: 13 Protein: 29

Camping Cookbook

FOIL PACKAGED CHICKEN BREAST

Intermediate | 50 minutes | Lunch and Dinner | 4 Servings

INGREDIENTS

- 1 lb. /453g of the Chicken breast (boneless, skinless, cubed)
- 2 Onions (diced)
- 8 oz. /226g of fresh mushrooms (sliced)
- 1 Yellow bell pepper (sliced)
- 1 Red bell pepper (sliced)
- 4 cloves of Garlic (sliced)
- 4 Potatoes (cubed)
- ¼ cup of Olive oil
- 1 Lemon (juiced)

COOKING STEPS

1. In a ziplock bag or a bowl, combine the chicken breast with onion, mushrooms, bell peppers, potatoes, and garlic, sprinkle with olive oil and lemon. Whisk to combine.
2. Divide the mixture evenly between four aluminum foil packets and cover each packet with a foil as well.
3. Cook for 40 minutes over a campfire or until potatoes are tender and chick opaque.

Nutrition:

Calories: 328 | Fat: 18 | Fiber: 3 | Carbs: 12 | Protein: 32

Camping Cookbook

LEMON GARLIC FOIL PACKET

Intermediate   25 minutes   Lunch and Dinner   4 Servings

INGREDIENTS

- 1 lb. /453g of Raw shrimp (peeled, deveined)
- 4 tbsp. of Butter
- 3 cloves of Garlic (minced)
- 1 tbsp. of Lemon zest
- 1 tbsp. of Lemon juice
- 1 tbsp. of Parsley (dried)
- ¼ tbsp. of Red pepper flakes
- Salt and pepper to taste

COOKING STEPS

1. Place the shrimp in the center of the foil packet then add butter and the rest ingredients.
2. Fold the foil and cook over a campfire for 8-10 minutes, then flip the packet and continue cooking for 3-5 minutes.
3. Serve on its own or in combination with a side dish of your choice.

Nutrition:

Calories: 256

Fat: 18

Fiber: 3

Carbs: 13

Protein: 35

Camping Cookbook

HOBO CHICKEN AND VEGETABLES

Intermediate | 35 minutes | Lunch and Dinner | 4 Servings

INGREDIENTS

- ✓ 1 lb. of chicken breast, skinless, boneless, cubed
- ✓ 1 onion, diced
- ✓ 1 pkg (8 oz.) of mushrooms
- ✓ 4 cloves of garlic, diced
- ✓ 4 small potatoes, cubed
- ✓ 1/4 cup of butter
- ✓ 1 lemon, juiced

COOKING STEPS

1. Combine the chicken, onion, mushrooms, garlic, and potatoes in a large bowl or zip-lock bag. Apply the lemon juice and blend well. Divide the mixture equally into four large pieces of aluminum foil, put the mixture in the middle and cover with butter slices.

2. Fold two ends of the foil, so that they cross in the middle and roll to lock them downwards. Roll inward into the mixture of the remaining two ends so that it is stable.

3. Put for approximately 40 minutes or until chicken is thoroughly cooked over the campfire with the seam side up. Remove from the fire and allow a few minutes to cool. Be very vigilant about opening foil pouches so that the steam does not fry you.

Nutrition:

Calories: 307 Fat: 9 Fiber: 6 Carbs: 21 Protein: 27

Camping Cookbook

GRILLED SALMON WITH LEMON

Camp Master | 30 minutes | Lunch and Dinner | 4 Servings

INGREDIENTS

- 1/2 cup of fresh lemon juice
- 1/4 cup of olive oil
- 1 small onion, finely chopped
- 1 clove of garlic, minced
- 2 tbsp. of dried dill
- Salmon
- Salt and black pepper to taste

COOKING STEPS

1. Lemon juice, oil, onion, garlic, dill salt, and pepper are mixed at home. Store in a securely packed bag and store until ready for use in the refrigerator or cooler. For longer storage, freeze.
2. At Camp: thaw, if frozen, marinade. Put the salmon in a shallow pan, pour the marinade over the salmon, and let stand for 20 minutes before frying.
3. Take the fish out and discard the marinade. Place on a grill rack with fish skin-side down. Cook for 10 minutes per inch of thickness over medium-hot heat, or until the fish is opaque and flakes easily with a fork.

Nutrition:

Calories: 278   Fat: 10   Fiber: 3   Carbs: 19   Protein: 28

Camping Cookbook

HAWAIIAN STYLE PORK CHOPS

Camp Master | 35 minutes | Lunch and Dinner | 4 Servings

INGREDIENTS

- 1 cup of pineapple juice
- 1 small onion, diced
- 3 tbsp. of soy sauce
- 2 tbsp. of brown sugar
- 1 tbsp. of sesame oil
- Boned pork chops
- Salt and black pepper to taste

COOKING STEPS

1. At Home: combine pineapple juice, onion, soy sauce, butter, sesame seed, salt, and pepper for the marinade. Add the marinade chops. Keep until fit for use in a cooler or refrigerator.

2. At Camp: cut the marinade chops and dump the marinade. On a finely oiled grill rack, cook over the medium-hot sun, rotating once, for 5 min per side or until an instant-read thermometer inserted into the middle of the chops reads 170 ° F.

Nutrition:

Calories: 264

Fat: 10

Fiber: 6

Carbs: 19

Protein: 28

Camping Cookbook

HERB-STUFFED GRILLED FISH

Camp Master | 35 minutes | Lunch and Dinner | 4 Servings

INGREDIENTS

- ✓ 2 tbsp. of olive oil
- ✓ Zest from 1 lime
- ✓ 4 fresh dill branches
- ✓ 4 green onions
- ✓ Canola oil
- ✓ 1 small clove garlic, crushed
- ✓ 2 fresh fish fillets
- ✓ Lime juice
- ✓ Salt and pepper to taste

COOKING STEPS

1. At Home: combine the garlic, olive oil, lime juice, and zest in a shallow dish. Store in the refrigerator or cooler in an airtight jar until ready for use. For longer storage, freeze.

2. At Camp: lime thaw sauce, if frozen. Pat fillets of dried fish with paper towels. Green onions and dills should be put along the length of one fish fillet. Cover with a second fillet; gently coat the fish with grease.

3. Wrap up in foil, securely safe. Cook for 10 minutes over medium-hot heat or on a finely oiled grill rack, or until the fish is opaque and quickly fork-flaked. Season with salt and pepper to taste. Serve with lime-sauce drizzled over cod.

Nutrition:

Calories 297   Fat 13   Fiber 5   Carbs 19   Protein 36

Camping Cookbook

PAN-FRIED POTATOES AND MUSHROOMS

Camp Master | 35 minutes | Lunch and Dinner | 4 Servings

INGREDIENTS

- 1 small onion, chopped
- 2 tbsp. of butter
- 2 cup potatoes, cooked and diced
- 1/2 cup of mushrooms
- 1 cup of cheddar cheese, shredded
- Salt and black pepper to taste

COOKING STEPS

1. Sauté the onion in the butter in a medium skillet over medium heat for 5 minutes or until tender. Connect the mushrooms and potatoes and finish cooking for 5 minutes.

2. Add seasonings, sprinkle with cheese, minimize pressure, cover and simmer until the cheese is melted for an additional 5 minutes. Immediately serve.

Nutrition:

Calories: 259

Fat: 13

Fiber: 9

Carbs: 27

Protein: 32

Camping Cookbook

SLOW-COOKED PULLED PORK

Camp Master | 35 minutes | Lunch and Dinner | 4 Servings

INGREDIENTS

- 1 cup of chili sauce
- 1/3 cup of Dijon mustard
- 1/3 cup of honey
- 2 tbsp. of chili powder
- 2 tbsp. of tomato paste
- 2 tbsp. of Worcestershire sauce
- 1 tbsp. of packed brown sugar
- 2 tbsp. of paprika
- 2 large clove garlic, minced
- 2 cup of sliced onion
- 3-4 lbs. of pork shoulder roast
- 2 cup of chopped apples
- Large ciabatta rolls, onion buns

COOKING STEPS

1. Mix the hot sauce, vinegar, butter, chili powder, tomato paste, Worcestershire sauce, brown sugar, paprika, and garlic together at home. Place or freeze in a closely sealed jar for longer storage.

2. At Camp: thaw, if frozen, sauce. Place the onions in the lower section of the Dutch oven. Place the pork over the onions and apples on top. Pour the sauce over the apples and beef.

3. Cover and simmer for 4 hours over medium heat or until the meat is tender and starting to fall apart. Take the meat from the oven and use forks to shred the meat. Serve with rolls as a garnish using the leftover sauce.

Nutrition:

Calories: 278 | Fat: 14 | Fiber: 9 | Carbs: 21 | Protein: 32

Camping Cookbook

Chapter 9. Soups and Stews

Camping Cookbook

HERB-STUFFED GRILLED FISH

Beginner | 80 minutes | Soups and Stews | 6 Servings

INGREDIENTS

- Spice packet
- 1 teaspoon of salt
- ½ teaspoon of freshly ground black pepper
- 2 ½ teaspoons of ground cumin
- 1 ½ teaspoon of chili powder
- 1 teaspoon of crushed chilies
- 1 tablespoon of paprika
- 1 tablespoon of dried oregano
- 1 cinnamon of stick
- 1 bay leaf
- 1 ½ pound of lean ground beef
- 1 large onion, chopped
- 3 cloves of garlic, chopped
- 2 (14.5-ounce) cans of diced tomatoes with liquid
- 1 (15-ounce) can of red kidney beans, rinsed

COOKING STEPS

1. At home, combine the necessary spices in a lidded container or a reusable bag.
2. At the campsite, place your 12-inch Dutch oven over 18 briquettes.
3. Sauté the ground beef until it is browned and drain any excess of grease.
4. Add the onion and cook until it is tender, then stir in the garlic. Add the spices and tomatoes.
5. Cover the pot, and arrange it with 16 briquettes underneath and 8 on top. Cook for 45 minutes, maintaining a temperature around 325°F.
6. Add the beans and cook for 15 more minutes. Remove the cinnamon stick and bay leaf before serving.

and drained
- ✓ 1 (15-ounce) can of black beans, rinsed and drained

Nutrition:

- Calories: 318
- Fat: 12
- Fiber: 5
- Carbs: 30
- Protein: 19

Camping Cookbook

POTATOES AND MEATBALLS

Beginner | 35 minutes | Soups and Stews | 4 Servings

INGREDIENTS

- ½ pound of hamburger meat
- ½ cup of carrots, chopped
- 5 small red potatoes, halved
- ½ onion, diced
- 1 package dry ranch dressing
- ½ tablespoon of salt
- ½ tablespoon of pepper

COOKING STEPS

1. Add salt and pepper to hamburger meat and divide the meat up into meatballs.
2. Place the meatballs on the foil.
3. Add the vegetables around the meatballs.
4. Season the meatballs and vegetables with dry ranch dressing.
5. Seal the foil packet, leaving room for steam.
6. Cook the packet for 30 to 35 minutes, or until the hamburger is cooked to your liking and vegetables are soft. Flip the packet after 15 minutes.
7. Open the packet carefully and enjoy.

Nutrition:

Calories: 338   Fat: 20   Fiber: 13   Carbs: 41   Protein: 49

Camping Cookbook

HODGE PODGE

Beginner | 55 minutes | Soups and Stews | 6 Servings

INGREDIENTS

- 1 ½ cups of fresh green beans, trimmed and snapped
- 1 ½ cups of fresh wax beans, trimmed and snapped
- 1 ½ cups of diced carrot
- 2 cups of cubed new potatoes
- ½ teaspoon of salt
- ¼ cup of salted butter
- ¼ cup of heavy cream
- 1 tablespoon of all-purpose flour
- 1 cup of whole milk
- Salt and pepper to taste

COOKING STEPS

1. Place the beans, carrots, potatoes, and salt in a saucepan and add just enough water to cover.
2. Simmer for 30–40 minutes, until all the vegetables are tender.
3. Stir in the butter and cream.
4. Whisk the flour into the milk and add it to the pot. Cook until thickened and season with salt and pepper to taste.

Nutrition:

Calories: 199   Fat: 12   Fiber: 5   Carbs: 18   Protein: 3

Camping Cookbook

CAMPFIRE CHICKEN AND DUMPLINGS

Intermediate | 55 minutes | Soups and Stews | 6 Servings

INGREDIENTS

- 1 whole fryer chicken, 4-5 pounds
- 4 stalks celery, sliced
- 1 large onion, diced
- 2 medium carrots, peeled and sliced
- 1 teaspoon of salt
- 1 teaspoon of black pepper
- 2 teaspoons of garlic powder
- 1 (14.5-ounce) can of low-sodium chicken broth

For the dumplings:

- 1 ½ cups of white whole wheat flour
- ½ teaspoon of salt
- 5 tablespoons of butter
- 1 egg
- ½ cup of milk
- 1 tablespoon of dried parsley

COOKING STEPS

1. Place a large Dutch oven over 18–20 briquettes. Add the chicken with enough water to just cover. Put in the celery, onion, carrots, salt, black pepper, and broth.
2. Bring the pot to a boil and then transfer it to less intense heat. Keep it simmering for an hour.
3. Meanwhile, prepare the dumpling batter. Combine the flour and salt and cut in the butter. Mix in the egg, milk, parsley, and pepper, and knead for about 5 minutes.
4. Carefully remove the chicken to a strainer and let it cool a little. Remove and discard any skin and fat, and pull the meat from the bones.
5. Skim the fat from the broth and add the cooked chicken back in. Taste the broth and add more seasonings if desired.
6. Pull off little bits of the dumpling dough and roll them into balls if desired. Drop them into the broth.
7. Cover the pot and bring it to a simmer. Cook, covered, for 20 minutes.

Nutrition:

Calories: 463 | Fat: 16 | Fiber: 5 | Carbs: 25 | Protein: 50

TOMATO CHICKPEA SOUP

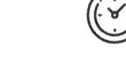

Intermediate | 40 minutes | Soups and Stews | 8 Servings

INGREDIENTS

- ¼ cup of extra-virgin olive oil
- 2 medium yellow onions, diced
- 1 stalk celery, diced
- 4 cloves of garlic, minced
- 1 bunch kale, trimmed and chopped (about 3 cups)
- 2 (28-ounce) cans of crushed tomatoes
- 1 quart of low-sodium vegetable stock
- 1 cup of basmati rice, rinsed
- ¼ cup of tomato paste
- 2 (15-ounce) cans of chickpeas, drained and rinsed
- 1 teaspoon of salt
- ½ teaspoon of black pepper
- Hot sauce or crushed chilies, to taste

COOKING STEPS

1. In your Dutch oven over 18 coals, warm the oil and sauté the onion and celery for 3–5 minutes. Stir in the garlic and cook until fragrant.
2. Add the kale, and stir a minute or two, until it begins to wilt.
3. Add the tomatoes, vegetable stock, and rice. Bring the mixture to a boil and let it simmer for 15–20 minutes.
4. Add the tomato paste, chickpeas, salt, pepper, and hot sauce. Cook to heat through, and serve.

Nutrition:

Calories: 323 | Fat: 9 | Fiber: 5 | Carbs: 52 | Protein: 11

SPICED LENTIL SOUP

Intermediate | 40 minutes | Soups and Stews | 8 Servings

INGREDIENTS

- Spice packet
- 2 teaspoons of ground turmeric
- 1 ½ teaspoon of ground cumin
- ¼ teaspoon of cinnamon
- ½ teaspoon of sea salt
- ½ teaspoon of black pepper
- Pinch red pepper flakes
- 2 tablespoons of extra virgin olive oil
- 1 large onion, diced
- 3 cloves of garlic, minced
- ¾ cup of red lentils, rinsed and drained
- 1 (15-ounce) can of diced tomatoes, with juices
- 1 (15 ounces) can of light coconut milk
- 1 quart of low-sodium

COOKING STEPS

1. At home, combine the spices in a small, lidded container, and seal.
2. In your Dutch oven over 18 coals, warm the oil and sauté the onion and garlic until tender.
3. Add the spices and the lentils and mix well. Continue cooking for another minute or two, but don't let the spices burn.
4. Add the tomatoes, coconut milk, and broth. Bring it to a boil and simmer, uncovered, for 20 minutes, or until the lentils are tender.
5. Add the spinach and lemon juice, and cook until the spinach wilts.

Camping Cookbook

- vegetable broth
- ✓ 3 cups of packed baby spinach
- ✓ 1 tablespoon of fresh lemon juice

Nutrition:

Calories: 254

Fat: 14

Fiber: 5

Carbs: 25

Protein: 7

Camping Cookbook

FIREMAN'S SPICY STEW

Camp Master | 95 minutes | Lunch and Dinner | 12 Servings

INGREDIENTS

- 1 teaspoon of oregano, dried
- 4 garlic cloves, minced
- 2 tablespoons of ground cumin
- 2 tablespoons of ground coriander
- 3 tablespoons of chili powder
- 1 can (14 ½ ounces each) of beef broth
- 3 cans (14 ½ ounces each) of stewed tomatoes, diced
- 4 cans (16 ounces each) of kidney beans, rinsed and drained
- 1 medium green pepper, chopped
- 2 medium onions, chopped
- 4 pounds (90%) of lean ground beef
- 2 tablespoons of olive oil

COOKING STEPS

1. Preheat your Dutch oven.
2. Using a pot, heat the olive oil over medium heat in your Dutch oven.
3. Add beef in batches and brown them, making sure to crumble the meat in the process until they are no longer pink.
4. Drain any excess oil and keep the meat on the side.
5. Add onions, green pepper, cook until fragrant, and shows a nice soft texture.
6. Re-introduce the meat to the oven and stir in the remaining ingredients.
7. Bring the mix to a boil and lower the heat. Simmer (covered) for about 1 and ½ hour until thoroughly cooked, and the flavors have blended in.
8. Enjoy!

Nutrition:

Calories: 443 | Protein: 27g | Fat: 27g | Carbs: 15g

CREAMY BACON AND POTATO SOUP

Camp Master 75 minutes Lunch and Dinner 4 Servings

INGREDIENTS

- ¼ teaspoon of pepper
- 1 teaspoon of salt
- 1 tablespoon of fresh chives, chopped
- ¼ cup of flour
- 1 cup of cheddar cheese, shredded
- 2 cups of water
- 2 cups of whole milk
- 1 onion, chopped
- 10 garlic cloves, minced
- 2 pounds of large russet potatoes, peeled and cut up into 1/2 inch pieces
- 6 piece of bacon slices
- 1 whole onion, chopped

COOKING STEPS

1. Preheat your Dutch oven.
2. Heat a pot over medium heat.
3. Add bacon and cook for about 10-15 minutes until crispy.
4. Transfer to a paper towel and drain excess grease.
5. Once cooled, crumble into small pieces.
6. Add onions to your pot alongside bacon grease.
7. Cook for about 5 minutes until tender, making sure to stir from time to time.
8. Add flour and remaining ingredients, stir cook for 3 minutes.
9. Add water and stir until everything is mixed well.
10. Add milk and stir, bring the mix to a boil over high heat.
11. Lower down the heat to medium-low and let the mixture simmer for about 15 minutes.
12. Make sure to keep stirring it in order to prevent the potatoes from burning.
13. Once done, serve in bowls with a topping of bacon crumbles, chopped chives, and cheddar.

Camping Cookbook

14. Enjoy!

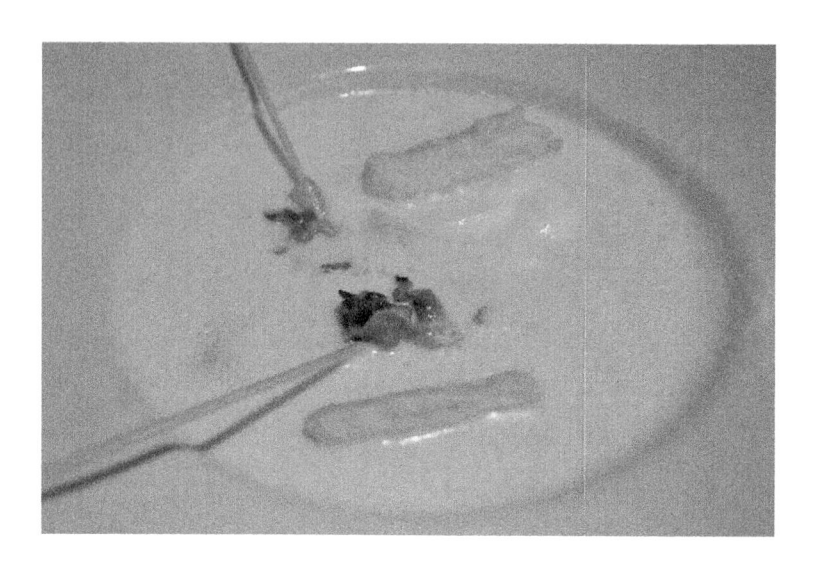

Nutrition:

Calories: 1549 kcal

Protein: 27g

Fat: 25g

Carbs: 53g

Camping Cookbook

Chapter 10. Snacks and Sides

Camping Cookbook

FOIL-PACK CHEESY FRIES

Beginner | 50 minutes | Snacks and Sides | 4 Servings

INGREDIENTS

- 2 tablespoons of real bacon bits, cooked
- 2 tablespoons of sliced green onions
- 4 slices of American cheese
- 1 tablespoon of butter, melted
- 1 bag (14 ounces) of frozen French fries

COOKING STEPS

1. Heat a charcoal grill or gas over medium heat, and then toss the melted butter with frozen French fries.
2. Tear off two foils and make foil boats. Put half of the fries in a single layer in the center of a foil then loosely fold around the edges to make a boat. Leave a large hole at the top for steam to escape through.
3. Repeat the procedure with the other foil and remaining fries. Now put the foil packet on the grill, cover, and cook for about 20 to 30 minutes but over indirect heat.
4. Stir once and cook until the fries are crispy. Top with 2 slices of cheese. If need be, cook for another 2 minutes or until baked through.
5. To serve, sprinkle with bacon bits, sliced green onions, and enjoy.

Nutrition:

Calories: 260 | Fat: 11 | Fiber: 7 | Carbs: 23 | Protein: 15

STREET CORN OVER THE CAMPFIRE

Beginner | 40 minutes | Snacks and Sides | 6 Servings

INGREDIENTS

- 2 fresh limes juiced
- 1 cup of parmesan cheese, freshly grated
- 1/2 cup of fresh cilantro, finely chopped
- 2 cups of sour cream
- 3/4 cup of mayo
- 6 ears of corn
- Chili powder to taste

COOKING STEPS

1. First, husk the corn or instead leave the ends on.
2. Grill the ears of corn over the campfire while occasionally turning to avoid burning the corn, until lightly charred.
3. Meanwhile, combine cilantro, sour cream, and mayo in a bowl.
4. Now remove the corn from the campfire and season with the mayo seasoning.
5. Allow the corn to cool then season with lime juice, then sprinkle cheese and some chili powder. Serve and enjoy.

Nutrition:

Calories: 291

Fat: 9

Fiber: 11

Carbs: 25

Protein: 18

Camping Cookbook

PESTO CATFISH PACKETS

Beginner | 25 minutes | Snacks and Sides | 8 Servings

INGREDIENTS

- Lime slices
- 1-pint cherry tomatoes cut into halves
- Black pepper, freshly ground
- 1 1/2 teaspoons of salt
- 1/2 cup of jarred pesto
- 8 (6-ounce) of catfish fillets
- 1/4 cup of extra-virgin olive oil

COOKING STEPS

1. Preheat the grill over medium-high heat, and then cut 8 pieces of foil, measuring approximately 8 by 11 inches.
2. Drizzle some oil over each piece of foil and put the catfish fillets on top of the oil. Spread about 1 tablespoon of pesto over each fish fillet.
3. Season with salt and pepper then top with lime slices and tomatoes.
4. Seal the packets and put them onto the preheated grill's rack. Cook until the fish is opaque, or for about 10 minutes.

Nutrition:

- Calories: 312
- Fat: 15
- Fiber: 8
- Carbs: 17
- Protein: 24

Camping Cookbook

FOIL PACKET HOT DOG

Beginner | 30 minutes | Snacks and Sides | 3 Servings

INGREDIENTS

- Salt and Pepper to taste
- Olive oil
- 3 fingerling potatoes, sliced thin
- 1/2 small onion, sliced thinly
- 1/2 red pepper sliced
- 1 pack Hebrew National Hot Dogs
- Aluminum foil

COOKING STEPS

1. Cut off large square aluminum foils and then put 1 to 3 hotdogs in each foil square.
2. Put sliced veggies on top of the hot dogs and drizzle oil over the hotdogs. Season the food with pepper and salt.
3. Now fold the aluminum foils into small envelopes and grill them on the preheated grill until the veggies are cooked through, in about 15 to 20 minutes.

Nutrition:

Calories: 260   Fat: 13   Fiber: 7   Carbs: 32   Protein: 24

Camping Cookbook

HERB STEAK FOIL PACKET

Intermediate   25 minutes   Snacks and Sides   1 Servings

INGREDIENTS

- 1 sprig of fresh rosemary
- 1/2 lemon
- 1 steak thin cut such as rib-eye
- Butter
- Olive Oil
- Pepper
- Dried Thyme
- Salt
- Asparagus, optional
- 2 sheets of Heavy Duty Foil

COOKING STEPS

1. First, heat the coals on your campfire or preheat your grill to medium-high heat.
2. Grease 12 by 12-inch heavy-duty foil with a dot of butter mixed with olive oil.
3. Season the steak with pepper and salt and then put it in the center of the heavy-duty foil. Season the meat with thyme, a slice of lemon, and rosemary leaves.
4. Place the lemon and fresh veggies next to the steak, dot with some butter, and then cover the mixture with the second piece of foil.
5. Completely seal the foil and then put the foil packet on the grill. Cook until the steak is cooked through, or for about 8 to 10 minutes; while flipping halfway during cook time.
6. Once done, allow the steak to sit for 2 to 3 minutes before opening the foil.

Nutrition:

Calories: 284   Fat: 14   Fiber: 9   Carbs: 19   Protein: 34

PARMESAN PEPPERED ASPARAGUS

Intermediate   30 minutes   Snacks and Sides   4 Servings

INGREDIENTS

- 1 pound of fresh asparagus, rough ends trimmed
- 2 tablespoons of olive oil
- ½ cup of parmesan cheese, preferably fresh
- 1 tablespoon of cracked black pepper
- 1 lemon, quartered
- 1 24"x24" or larger piece of greased aluminum foil

COOKING STEPS

1. Packet fold style: Tent
2. Layout the asparagus spears on the foil.
3. Drizzle with the olive oil and toss gently.
4. Sprinkle with parmesan cheese, cracked black pepper, and lemon juice. Add any remaining lemon quarters to the top.
5. Create a tent style fold and add it to your heat source.
6. Cook for 25 minutes, or until the asparagus spears are tender.

Nutrition:

Calories: 221   Fat: 10   Fiber: 3   Carbs: 19   Protein: 11

Camping Cookbook

FULLY LOADED BAKED POTATOES

Intermediate | 40 minutes | Snacks and Sides | 4 Servings

INGREDIENTS

- 4 medium-sized baking potatoes, cubed
- 1 tablespoon of olive oil or butter
- 1 cup of cooked bacon crumbles
- ½ cup of onion, diced
- ½ cup of white mushrooms, sliced
- ½ cup of tomato, diced
- ¼ cup of canned green chilies
- ½ cup of Muenster cheese, cubed
- ½ cup of cheddar cheese, cubed
- 1 teaspoon of salt
- 1 teaspoon of paprika
- ¼ cup of scallions, sliced (optional)
- Sour cream for garnish (optional)
- 4 16x16 or larger piece of greased aluminum foil

COOKING STEPS

1. Packet fold style: Tent

2. To a bowl or other container, add the potatoes, olive oil, and cooked bacon. Toss well.

3. Transfer equal amounts of the potatoes to each piece of aluminum foil.

4. Top with onion, white mushrooms, tomatoes, green chilies, Muenster cheese, cheddar cheese, salt and paprika.

5. Create a tent style fold with each packet before adding to your heat source.

6. Cook for 30 minutes, or until potatoes are tender.

7. Garnish with fresh chopped scallions and sour cream, if desired.

Nutrition:

Calories: 229   Fat: 10   Fiber: 9   Carbs: 23   Protein: 29

RUSTIC WHOLE CARROTS

Intermediate • 50 minutes • Snacks and Sides • 4 Servings

INGREDIENTS

- 1 pound of whole multi-colored carrots, fronds trimmed
- 2 tablespoons of olive oil
- 2 tablespoons of honey
- 2 fresh sprigs of rosemary
- 1 teaspoon of cracked black pepper
- ½ teaspoon of salt
- 1 16"x16" or larger piece of greased aluminum foil

COOKING STEPS

1. Packet fold style: Tent
2. In a bowl, combine the carrots with the olive oil and honey. Toss to coat well.
3. Add the carrots to the aluminum foil.
4. Season with rosemary sprigs, cracked black pepper, and salt.
5. Create a tent style fold and add it to your heat source.
6. Cook for 40 minutes, or until carrots are tender.

Nutrition:

Calories: 209   Fat: 8   Fiber: 7   Carbs: 15   Protein: 5

Camping Cookbook

BEST CORN CASSEROLE

Camp Master | 45 minutes | Snacks and Sides | 4 Servings

INGREDIENTS

- 4 cups of fresh corn kernels
- ½ cup of tomato, diced
- ¼ cup of canned green chilies
- 1 cup of heavy cream or whole milk
- ¼ cup of butter, cubed
- 1 cup of mild cheddar cheese, shredded or cubed
- 1 teaspoon of oregano
- 1 teaspoon of garlic powder
- 1 teaspoon of pepper
- 1 teaspoon of salt
- 1 24"x24" or larger piece of greased aluminum foil

COOKING STEPS

1. Packet fold style: Tent.

2. In a large bowl or another container, combine all of the ingredients including the corn kernels, tomatoes, green chilies, heavy cream, butter, cheddar cheese, oregano, garlic powder, pepper, and salt.

3. Transfer the ingredients to the aluminum foil.

4. Create a tent-style foil and add it to your heat source.

5. Cook for 30-35 minutes.

Nutrition:

Calories: 223   Fat: 9   Fiber: 7   Carbs: 19   Protein: 5

SIDEKICK CHEESE FRIES

Camp Master | **50 minutes** | **Snacks and Sides** | **4 Servings**

INGREDIENTS

- 1/12 ounce package of frozen French fry potatoes
- 2 tablespoons of olive oil
- 1 teaspoon of Cajun seasoning
- 1 teaspoon of pepper
- 1 teaspoon of salt
- 1 ½ cups of sharp cheddar cheese, shredded
- ½ cup of scallions, sliced
- 1 24x24 or larger piece of greased aluminum foil

COOKING STEPS

1. Packet fold style: Tent.
2. In a bowl or other container, combine the potatoes with the olive oil, Cajun seasoning, pepper, and salt.
3. Transfer the potatoes to the aluminum foil.
4. Top with cheddar cheese and create a tent style fold before adding to the heat source.
5. Cook for 35-40 minutes.
6. Garnish with fresh scallions, if desired.

Nutrition:

Calories: 257 | Fat: 12 | Fiber: 3 | Carbs: 23 | Protein: 16

Camping Cookbook

CREAMY STUFFED JALAPENOS

Camp Master   40 minutes   Snacks and Sides   4 Servings

INGREDIENTS

- 12 jalapeno peppers, split in half and seeded
- 1-8 ounce of package cream cheese, softened
- 1 cup of Monterey jack cheese, shredded
- ¼ cup of fresh cilantro, minced
- 12 bacon strips, cut in half
- 1 24"x24" or larger piece of greased aluminum foil

COOKING STEPS

1. Packet fold style: Flat
2. In a bowl, combine the cream cheese, Monterey jack cheese, and fresh cilantro.
3. Scoop equal amounts of the cheese into each jalapeno pepper half.
4. Wrap each jalapeno pepper half in half a slice of bacon.
5. Place the peppers in the center of the aluminum foil and create a flat style fold.
6. Add to your heat source and cook for 25-30 minutes, or until bacon and stuffing are cooked.

Nutrition:

Calories: 207   Fat: 11   Fiber: 3   Carbs: 18   Protein: 29

Camping Cookbook

GARLICKY CHEESE BREAD

Camp Master | 40 minutes | Snacks and Sides | 4 Servings

INGREDIENTS

- ✓ 1 can refrigerated of crescent or biscuit dough
- ✓ 1 ½ cup of Colby Jack cheese, shredded
- ✓ 3 tablespoons of butter, cubed
- ✓ 2 teaspoons of garlic powder
- ✓ 2 teaspoons of parsley
- ✓ 1 teaspoon of salt
- ✓ 1 teaspoon of pepper
- ✓ 1 24x24 or larger piece of greased aluminum foil

COOKING STEPS

1. Packet fold style: Tent.
2. Cut each biscuit into four pieces and add to a bowl.
3. Add in the Colby jack cheese, butter, garlic powder, parsley, salt, and pepper. Toss to mix.
4. Add the dough pieces to the aluminum foil and create a tent style fold before adding to your heat source.
5. Cook for 30 minutes, or until bread is golden and cooked through.

Nutrition:

Calories: 256   Fat: 13   Fiber: 8   Carbs: 23   Protein: 17

Chapter 11. Desserts and Drinks

Camping Cookbook

DECONSTRUCTED PEACH CHEESECAKE

Beginner | 40 minutes | Desserts and Drinks | 4 Servings

INGREDIENTS

- 2 peaches, halved, pitted
- 7 tablespoons of honey, plus some for drizzling
- 1 teaspoon of vanilla
- 1 cup of cream cheese
- 10 graham crackers

COOKING STEPS

1. Crush graham crackers and divide among four plates.

2. Mix honey and vanilla, brush peaches with the mixture.

3. Mix remaining honeyed vanilla with cream cheese and set aside.

4. Thread peaches onto two sticks, and cook 6" above fire until browned.

5. Dollop a quarter of cream cheese on each serving of graham crackers. Drizzle with honey, if desired.

6. Slice peaches, place on top of cream cheese, and serve.

Nutrition:

Calories: 218

Fat: 9

Fiber. 7

Carbs: 20

Protein: 12

Camping Cookbook

CINNAMON APPLE WITH BUTTERY NUT TOPPING

Beginner | 40 minutes | Desserts and Drinks | 4 Servings

INGREDIENTS

- 4 red apples
- ½ teaspoon of cinnamon
- ½ teaspoon of nutmeg
- 8 butter cookies
- ½ cup of walnuts, chopped
- ½ cup of raisins
- 4 tablespoons of brown sugar
- Vegetable oil
- Whipped cream topping (optional)
-

COOKING STEPS

1. Slice apples in half, remove the core, sprinkle with cinnamon, nutmeg, and brown sugar.

2. Heat grill to medium-high and coat grate with vegetable oil.

3. Place apple halves on a wire rack, grill for 10 minutes or until brown sugar caramelizes, and apple is fork-tender.

4. Place butter biscuits on the grill for a minute to warm, remove, and rough chop.

5. Plate grilled apples, top with nuts, raisins, and hot butter cookies.

6. Serve warm with whipped cream topping if desired.

Nutrition:

Calories: 201

Fat: 6

Fiber: 11

Carbs: 19

Protein: 9

Camping Cookbook

GRILLED PINEAPPLE AND MARASCHINO CHERRY POUND CAKE

Beginner | 40 minutes | Desserts and Drinks | 4 Servings

INGREDIENTS

- ½ pineapple, skin removed
- 1 jar of Maraschino cherries
- 1 teaspoon of cinnamon
- 4 skewers
- Vegetable oil
- 1 pound of cake

COOKING STEPS

1. Slice your pineapple into 1" chunks and sprinkle with cinnamon.

2. Thread pineapple chunks and maraschino cherries onto skewers.

3. Place grate over indirect heat and brush grate with vegetable oil.

4. Grill pineapple until it begins to get a nice brown caramelization and begins to char.

5. Slice up your pound cake and serve pineapple and cherries on top.

Nutrition:

Calories: 211

Fat: 10

Fiber: 6

Carbs: 23

Protein: 14

Camping Cookbook

PARMESAN PEPPERED ASPARAGUS

Beginner | 40 minutes | Desserts and Drinks | 4 Servings

INGREDIENTS

- 1 package jumbo of marshmallows
- 2 cups of Rice Krispies Cereal
- ¾ cup of milk chocolate chips

COOKING STEPS

1. Combine cereal with chocolate chips in a wide dish.
2. Skewer marshmallow onto the end of the stick.
3. Cook over open fire until marshmallow browns and becomes sticky.
4. Now, roll the sticky marshmallow in Rice Krispies and chocolate chips, and enjoy!

Nutrition:

Calories: 231

Fat: 8

Fiber: 9

Carbs: 29

Protein: 14

Camping Cookbook

GRILLED SPICED PINEAPPLE

Intermediate | 40 minutes | Desserts and Drinks | 4 Servings

INGREDIENTS

- ½ pineapple, skin removed
- 1 teaspoon of cinnamon
- Vegetable oil
- Milk chocolate chips (optional)
- 4 skewers

COOKING STEPS

1. Slice your pineapple into 1" chunks and sprinkle with cinnamon.

2. Thread pineapple chunks onto skewers. If using wooden skewers, make sure to soak them in water for at least 30 minutes before using.

3. Place grate over indirect heat and brush grate with vegetable oil.

4. Grill pineapple until it begins to get a nice brown caramelization and begins to char.

5. Serve warm. Sprinkle with chocolate chips, if desired.

Nutrition:

Calories: 202   Fat: 12   Fiber: 10   Carbs: 21   Protein: 13

Camping Cookbook

CHARRED PEACHES

Intermediate | 15 minutes | Desserts and Drinks | 4 Servings

INGREDIENTS

- 4 peaches, halved, pitted and skin removed
- 1 teaspoon of cinnamon
- 1 tablespoon of brown sugar
- Vegetable oil
- Whipped cream topping, optional

COOKING STEPS

1. 1. Sprinkle peaches halves with cinnamon.

2. Place grate over indirect heat and brush grate with vegetable oil.

3. Grill peaches face down for 2-3 minutes until heated through and lightly charred.

4. Flip over and sprinkle with brown sugar. Grill for 1 to 2 minutes more or until brown sugar is melted and starting to caramelize and peaches are tender.

5. Serve with the whipped cream topping, if desired.

Nutrition:

Calories: 207

Fat: 9

Fiber: 5

Carbs: 23

Protein: 12

Camping Cookbook

ORANGE CUPCAKES

Intermediate | 30 minutes | Desserts and Drinks | 6 Servings

Cooking Method: Foil wrapping

INGREDIENTS

- 6 oranges
- Box of cupcake mix
- A container of cream cheese frosting

COOKING STEPS

1. Cut the top 1/3 off from the oranges.
2. Scoop out the meat of the orange, so you have a hollow shell.
3. Whip up the cupcake mix per the directions on the box.
4. Fill each orange 2/3 of the way full with cupcake mix.
5. Place the top on the orange and wrap it in foil, so the top is held in place.
6. Place the foil-wrapped orange in the embers of the fire and bake for 10 to 20 minutes, or until the cupcake is cooked all the way through.
7. Let cool.
8. Frost and enjoy.

Nutrition:

Calories: 249　　Fat: 9　　Fiber: 11　　Carbs: 25　　Protein: 11

Camping Cookbook

OREO PUDDING PIE

Intermediate   40 minutes   Desserts and Drinks   6/8 Servings

INGREDIENTS

- 1 graham cracker pie crust
- 4 cups of milk
- A can of whipped cream
- 1 package of Oreo cookies
- 1 box of instant vanilla pudding
- 1 box of instant chocolate pudding

COOKING STEPS

1. Make the vanilla pudding by adding 2 cups of milk to the mix and whisking it for 3 minutes. Let it sit for 5 minutes to set.

2. Do the same with the chocolate pudding. You can make it while you're waiting for the vanilla pudding to set.

3. Fill the bottom half of the graham cracker crust with vanilla pudding.

4. Fill in the rest of the way with chocolate pudding.

5. Cover the top of the pie with whipped cream.

6. Crumble Oreo cookies over the top.

7. Cover with aluminum foil and let chill in an ice chest until serving time.

Nutrition:

Calories: 271   Fat: 15   Fiber: 5   Carbs: 27   Protein: 19

Camping Cookbook

PERSONAL FRUIT PIES

Camp Master | 40 minutes | Desserts and Drinks | 4/6 Servings

Cooking Method: Skillet on a grill

INGREDIENTS

- ✓ 1 can of instant biscuit mix
- ✓ 1 can of pie filling
- ✓ Whipped cream or powdered sugar

COOKING STEPS

1. Roll each biscuit out until it's flat.
2. Place 3 teaspoons of your favorite pie filling in the center of the biscuit.
3. Fold the edges up to cover the filling.
4. Cook in a skillet over the campfire or the barbecue grill. The pies are done when they're a golden brown color.
5. Top with whipped cream or powdered sugar and enjoy.

Nutrition:

Calories: 212

Fat: 8

Fiber: 3

Carbs: 19

Protein: 11

Camping Cookbook

PINEAPPLE DONUT DELIGHT

Camp Master | 22 minutes | Desserts and Drinks | 1 Servings

Cooking Method: Foil wrapping

INGREDIENTS

- 1 unfrosted cake donut
- ½ cup of pineapple chunks
- 1 tablespoon of butter
- 2 tablespoons of brown sugar
- ½ teaspoon of cinnamon

COOKING STEPS

1. Break donut into pieces and place on a piece of foil.
2. Melt butter and add brown sugar and cinnamon to it. Spread it out across the top of the donut.
3. Add pineapple chunks to the top.
4. Wrap in foil.
5. Cook for 8 to 12 minutes by placing the foil packet directly in hot coals.
6. Let cool for 10 minutes and serve warm.

Nutrition:

Calories: 259

Fat: 12

Fiber: 11

Carbs: 37

Protein: 16

Camping Cookbook

ROCKY ROAD CONES

Camp Master Cooking Method | **22 minutes Foil Wrapping** | **Desserts and Drinks** | **1 Servings**

INGREDIENTS

- 1 sugar cone
- A handful of marshmallows
- Chocolate chips
- 1 tablespoon of chunky peanut butter

COOKING STEPS

1. Add peanut butter to the inside of the cone.
2. Fill with marshmallows and chocolate chips.
3. Wrap the cone in aluminum foil.
4. Place foil wrap in the campfire for 5 minutes.
5. Flip over and leave in the campfire an additional 5 minutes.
6. Remove from the campfire and let cool for 5 minutes.
7. Unwrap and enjoy. Be careful because the marshmallow and chocolate can get really hot.

Nutrition:

Calories: 196

Fat: 18

Fiber: 3

Carbs: 15

Protein: 9

Camping Cookbook

S'MORES

Camp Master Cooking Method | **25 minutes** | **Desserts and Drinks Skewer** | **1 Servings**

INGREDIENTS

- ✓ Graham crackers
- ✓ Jumbo marshmallows
- ✓ Milk chocolate bars

COOKING STEPS

1. Place a jumbo marshmallow on a skewer and cook it over the campfire until golden brown.

2. Place a piece of chocolate and the toasted marshmallow on a piece of graham cracker and create a sandwich by placing another piece of graham cracker over the top.

3. Wait 60 seconds, so the chocolate starts to melt, and the marshmallow cools a bit and enjoy.

Nutrition:

Calories: 187

Fat: 14

Fiber: 3

Carbs: 15

Protein: 9

Camping Cookbook

STRAWBERRY S'MORES

Camp Master Cooking Method | 20 minutes Skewer | Desserts and Drinks | 1 Servings

INGREDIENTS

- ✓ Graham crackers
- ✓ Jumbo marshmallows
- ✓ Milk chocolate bars
- ✓ Sliced strawberries

COOKING STEPS

1. Place a jumbo marshmallow on a skewer and cook it over the campfire until golden brown.

2. Place a piece of chocolate, a few strawberry pieces, and the toasted marshmallow on a piece of graham cracker and create a sandwich by placing another piece of graham cracker over the top.

3. Wait 60 seconds, so the chocolate starts to melt, and the marshmallow cools a bit and enjoy.

Nutrition:

Calories: 188

Fat: 14

Fiber: 7

Carbs: 15

Protein: 10

Camping Cookbook

Chapter 12. Backcountry Camping

Camping Cookbook

Backcountry Camping Essentials

- Spatula: a wok spatula or similar utensil in wood, bamboo, or silicone for stirring and deglazing. A wok spatula is angled on the bottom, with one curved side and one straight side, for getting into corners. While you can use metal utensils, they can scratch the enameled surface if you're not careful.

- Tongs: silicone-tipped long tongs for turning foods as you brown them prove more useful than a spatula. The deep sides of a Dutch oven keep splattering to a minimum, but they also make it easy to burn your arms if your utensils don't reach easily into the pot.

- Potholders: oven mitts or square potholders are essential. Standard Dutch ovens don't come with stay-cool handles, and even the stay-cool lid knob will heat up if you use your pot in the oven.

- Fry gear: if you plan to deep-fry in your Dutch oven, invest in a deep-fry thermometer and a "spider," a long-handled, basket-shaped strainer for removing food from the oil. A rack that fits in a sheet pan is great for draining foods after frying.

- Steamer: collapsible metal or flexible silicone steamer inserts will let you steam green vegetables, eggs, and potatoes. I like silicone inserts since they don't scratch my pots, but some of the collapsible metal models now come with silicone-coated feet, which also work well.

- Colander: if you want to cook pasta or boil potatoes in your Dutch oven, you'll need a colander or at least a large strainer to drain off the water.

- Fat separator: when you braise meat, it'll release fat into your sauce. You can simply blot or spoon this off, but a fat separator (which looks similar to a liquid measuring cup) does a more thorough job.

Camping Cookbook

Chapter 13. Breakfast

Camping Cookbook

PARMESAN PEPPERED ASPARAGUS

Beginner | 50 minutes | Breakfast | 4 Servings

INGREDIENTS

- 6 potatoes, medium
- 8 slices of bacon
- Butter, as required
- 6 organic eggs, large
- Pepper & salt to taste
- 1 onion, medium, diced
- Fresh parsley, chopped, optional

COOKING STEPS

1. Cook the potatoes in boiling salted water (with their skins) for a couple of minutes, until done, over moderately high heat.

2. Let cool, leave skins on or peel and then, slice or cube into pieces.

3. Cut the bacon into small bite-sized pieces and fry until desired crispness is achieved, over medium heat. Place it on a paper towel to drain.

4. Add approximately 2 tablespoons of butter to the bacon fat; fry the onions, for 2 to 3 minutes, until turn transparent.

5. Add potatoes to the hot pan, fry for a minute or two, until crust forms, and then, add the bacon pieces.

6. Crack eggs into the potatoes; cook and scramble well. Sprinkle with pepper and salt to taste. Just before serving, garnish your recipe with freshly chopped parsley. Serve warm and enjoy.

Nutrition:

Calories: 430 | Fat: 26 | Fiber: 14 | Carbs: 15 | Protein: 34

CAMPING BREAKFAST SANDWICH

Beginner | 30 minutes | Breakfast | 4 Servings

INGREDIENTS

- 4 slices of cheddar cheese
- 2 cups of BBQ pulled pork, leftover
- 4 sourdough of English muffins
- 4 organic eggs, large-sized
- Butter, as required

COOKING STEPS

1. Over moderate heat in a cast-iron saucepan, preferably medium-sized, heat up some of the butter until melted and then, crisp up the English muffins until turn golden and crispy, for a minute or two, set aside until ready to use.

2. Reheat the leftover pork in the same skillet, set aside and then, fry the eggs.

3. Fill the English muffin with approximately ½ cup of the pulled pork followed by a runny egg and a cheddar cheese slice. Using an aluminum foil, wrap, and place over the fire for a minute, until the cheese is completely melted.

4. Serve hot and enjoy.

Nutrition:

Calories: 680

Fat: 28

Fiber: 10

Carbs: 15

Protein: 34

Camping Cookbook

MAPLE SRIRACHA CHICKEN KABOBS

Beginner | 30 minutes | Breakfast | 4 Servings

INGREDIENTS

- 2 chicken breasts, large, cubed
- 1 pineapple, cubed
- ¼ cup of soy sauce
- 1 tablespoon of Sriracha sauce
- ¼ cup of maple syrup
- 1 red bell pepper, cubed

COOKING STEPS

1. Whisk the soy sauce with sriracha sauce, and maple syrup in a medium-sized mixing bowl; set aside.

2. In a large re-sealable plastic bag, whisk the cubed chicken breasts with the prepared marinate; massage the chicken pieces well until nicely coated.

3. Let rest in the ice chest for an hour.

4. Once the marinating part is done, soak the wooden skewers in water for a couple of minutes.

5. Skewer the coated chicken pieces with pineapple and red bell pepper on to the soaked skewer.

6. Grill for 7 to 10 minutes, until the chicken is cooked through.

7. Serve hot and enjoy.

Nutrition:

Calories: 117   Fat: 2   Fiber: 10   Carbs: 15   Protein: 15

Camping Cookbook

DUTCH OVEN CHICKEN AND DUMPLINGS

Beginner | 80 minutes | Breakfast | 8 Servings

INGREDIENTS

- 1 fryer/broiler chicken (approximately 2 ½ to 3 pounds), chunked or shredded
- 4 celery ribs, sliced
- 1 teaspoon of celery seed
- 3 carrots, medium, sliced
- 1 cup of onion, chopped
- 2 teaspoons of sage, rubbed, divided
- ¾ cup plus 2 tablespoons of milk
- 3 cups of baking/biscuit mix
- 1 tablespoon of fresh parsley, minced
- 3 cups of water
- ¼ teaspoon of pepper
- 1 teaspoon of salt

COOKING STEPS

1. Fill a Dutch oven with chicken and water, cover and bring it to a boil, over moderate heat.
2. Once done, decrease the heat to simmer, continue to cook for 25 to 30 minutes, until the chicken is fork-tender.
3. Remove the chicken from kettle, bone, and cube.
4. Return the chicken along with the celery seed, celery, onion, carrots, 1 teaspoon of sage, pepper, and salt to the kettle, bring the mixture to a boil. Once done, decrease the heat.
5. Cover and let simmer until the vegetables are tender, for 45 to 60 minutes.
6. For Dumplings: just combine the milk with biscuit mix, leftover sage and parsley, forming a stiff batter.
7. Using tablespoonful, carefully drop it into the hot chicken mixture.
8. Cover and let simmer for 12 to 15 minutes. Serve hot and enjoy.

Nutrition:

Calories: 69 | Fat: 2 | Fiber: 1 | Carbs: 15 | Protein: 2

SPAGHETTI SANDWICH

Beginner | 20 minutes | Breakfast | 1 Servings

INGREDIENTS

- ✓ 1 cup of spaghetti sauce, ready-to-serve
- ✓ ½ cup of spaghetti pasta (about ½ cup per sandwich)
- ✓ 2 slices of bread per sandwich
- ✓ ¾ cup of butter
- ✓ 2 teaspoons of Italian seasoning
- ✓ 2 teaspoons of garlic powder or crushed garlic

COOKING STEPS

1. Prepare the campfire.
2. Cook the spaghetti in a skillet filled with salted water; drain and set aside. (You can also pre-cook it at home.)
3. Combine the spaghetti and spaghetti sauce in a bowl. Set aside for 5–10 minutes.
4. In another bowl, combine the garlic, butter, and Italian seasoning.
5. Grease both sides of the pie iron with cooking spray.
6. Spread garlic butter over a slice of bread and place it butter side down at the pie iron bottom.
7. Add ½ cup of spaghetti and top with another garlic-buttered bread slice.
8. Close and latch the pie iron.
9. Place the pie iron over the coals and cook for 6–8 minutes, flipping every 1–2 minutes.
10. Remove the pie iron from the coals. Serve warm.

Nutrition:

Calories: 1944 | Fat: 152 | Fiber: 5 | Carbs: 126 | Protein: 23

LOBSTER ROLL SANDWICH

Beginner | 25 minutes | Breakfast | 4 Servings

INGREDIENTS

- Mayonnaise to taste
- Lemon juice to taste
- Hot sauce to taste
- Salt and pepper to taste
- ½ cup of butter or 1 stick
- ½ cup of lobster chunks per sandwich
- 2 slices of white bread or English Muffin Toasting Bread

COOKING STEPS

1. Prepare the campfire.
2. Melt at least 1 stick of butter in a skillet; this is sufficient to make 4 sandwiches.
3. Remove from heat and add the lobster. Mix in the lemon juice and one or two dashes of hot sauce. Toss well.
4. Place one slice of bread at the bottom of the pie iron. Spread mayonnaise and add lobster meat on top.
5. Spread mayonnaise over another bread slice and place it on top.
6. Close and latch the pie iron.
7. Place the pie iron over the coals and cook on both sides until golden brown.
8. Remove the pie iron from the coals. Serve warm.

Nutrition:

Calories: 267

Fat: 24

Fiber: 5

Carbs: 9

Protein: 2

Camping Cookbook

BAKED BEANS BROWN BREAD SANDWICH

Beginner 25 minutes Breakfast 1 Servings

INGREDIENTS

- 1 can of brown bread (optionally with raisins)
- 2 strips of bacon for each sandwich
- 1 can of baked beans
- Finely chopped onion (optional)

COOKING STEPS

1. Prepare the campfire.
2. Add the bacon to a skillet and cook on both sides until crispy. Drain over paper towels and set aside.
3. Slice the brown bread into ½-inch-thick slices.
4. Grease both sides of the pie iron with butter, vegetable oil, or cooking spray.
5. Place one slice of bread at the bottom of the pie iron. Add two strips of bacon, crumbling them as needed.
6. Add a large spoonful of beans and chopped onion.
7. Place another slice of bread on top.
8. Close and latch the pie iron.
9. Place the pie iron over the coals and cook on both sides until golden brown.
10. Remove the pie iron from the coals. Serve warm.

Nutrition:

Calories 1294 Fat: 34 Fiber: 5 Carbs: 212 Protein: 47

EGG SAUSAGE SANDWICH

Intermediate 15 minutes Breakfast 4 Servings

INGREDIENTS

- 1 slice cheddar cheese
- A dough of 1 biscuit
- 1 sausage patty or two strips of bacon (optional)
- 1 egg

COOKING STEPS

1. Prepare the campfire.
2. Preheat the pie iron and grease both sides with butter, vegetable oil, or cooking spray.
3. Place the dough at the bottom of the pie iron.
4. Close and latch the pie iron.
5. Place the pie iron over the coals and cook for about 2 minutes. Flip and cook for 2 more minutes until brown on top.
6. Add the bacon or sausage to a skillet and cook on both sides until crispy and evenly brown.
7. Slice the cooked dough, add the sausage and cheese, and set aside.
8. Open the pie iron, crack the egg into it and without closing, cook over the coals until the egg white starts to set.
9. Close the pie iron, flip it, and cook until the egg is cooked to your satisfaction.
10. Top the biscuit with the cooked egg and serve warm.

Nutrition:

Calories: 653 Fat: 49 Fiber: 5 Carbs: 26 Protein: 5

TURKEY EGG SANDWICH

Intermediate   15 minutes   Breakfast   4 Servings

INGREDIENTS

- 2 slices of turkey
- 2 slices of ham
- 2 slices of cheddar cheese
- 1 egg
- 2 slices of bread
- 1 tablespoon of milk
- Powdered sugar to taste

COOKING STEPS

1. Prepare the campfire.
2. Grease both sides of the pie iron with butter, vegetable oil, or cooking spray.
3. Lightly beat the eggs in a bowl. Mix in the milk.
4. Evenly coat the bread with the egg mixture.
5. Place one slice of bread at the bottom of the pie iron. Add the ham, turkey, and cheese on top.
6. Place the other slice of bread on top.
7. Close and latch the pie iron.
8. Place the pie iron over the coals and cook for about 5 minutes. Flip and cook for 5 more minutes.
9. Remove the pie iron from the coals. Serve warm with powdered sugar on top.

Nutrition:

Calories: 556   Fat: 30   Fiber: 5   Carbs: 24   Protein: 45

CLASSIC TOMATO CHEESE SANDWICH

| Intermediate | 15 minutes | Breakfast | 1 Servings |

INGREDIENTS

- 1 slice of mozzarella
- 2 slices of tomato (you can also use canned tomatoes)
- 3 basil leaves
- 2 slices bread
- Balsamic vinegar glaze

COOKING STEPS

1. Prepare the campfire.
2. Grease both sides of the pie iron with butter, vegetable oil, or cooking spray.
3. Place one slice of bread at the bottom of the pie iron. Add the tomato and cheese slices.
4. Add the basil leaves on top. Drizzle with balsamic vinegar glaze.
5. Place the other slice of bread on top. Close and latch the pie iron.
6. Place the pie iron over the coals and cook for about 3 minutes. Flip and cook for 2–3 more minutes until evenly brown.
7. Remove the pie iron from the coals. Serve warm.

Nutrition:

Calories: 174

Fat: 5

Fiber: 5

Carbs: 20

Protein: 10

HOT DOGS

Intermediate | 35 minutes | Breakfast | 4 Servings

INGREDIENTS

- 2 hot dogs
- ½ red pepper, sliced
- ½ green pepper, sliced
- ½ onion, sliced
- 1 teaspoon of olive oil
- 2 hot dog buns
- Mustard, to taste

COOKING STEPS

1. Place hot dogs on the foil.
2. Add peppers and onions.
3. Drizzle with olive oil.
4. Fold foil packet up tightly.
5. Cook in the campfire for 15 to 20 minutes, or until hot dogs are cooked all the way through.
6. Remove from fire and open foil packet.
7. Place hot dogs, peppers, and onions on hot dog buns.
8. Season with mustard, to taste.

Nutrition:

Calories: 291

Fat: 13

Fiber: 7

Carbs: 39

Protein: 21

KOREAN STEAK

Intermediate | 30 minutes | Breakfast | 4 Servings

INGREDIENTS

- ½ pound steak, sliced
- 1 scallion, sliced thinly
- 2 tablespoons of soy sauce
- 1 tablespoon of rice vinegar
- 1 tablespoon of brown sugar
- 1 teaspoon of ginger, grated
- 1 teaspoon of sesame oil
- Red pepper, to taste

COOKING STEPS

1. Combine sauce ingredients in a bowl and stir together.
2. Place scallion and steak on the foil.
3. Pour sauce over the top.
4. Fold foil packet up tightly.
5. Cook for 15 to 20 minutes, or until the steak is cooked to your liking.
6. Let sit for 5 minutes before eating.

Nutrition:

Calories: 358

Fat: 16

Fiber: 10

Carbs: 27

Protein: 46

LEMON THYME STEAK AND ASPARAGUS

Intermediate | 25 minutes | Breakfast | 4 Servings

INGREDIENTS

- 1 sirloin steak
- 5 asparagus spears
- 1 lemon, sliced
- 2 teaspoons of thyme
- 1 teaspoon of butter
- 1 teaspoon of olive oil
- Salt and pepper, to taste

COOKING STEPS

1. Place steak on the foil.
2. Place asparagus spears around steak.
3. Season the steak with salt, pepper, and thyme.
4. Place butter on the asparagus.
5. Drizzle olive oil over everything.
6. Place lemon slices over steak.
7. Close foil packet, leaving room for steam.
8. Cook for 12 to 15 minutes, or until the steak is cooked to your liking.
9. Let sit for 5 minutes before opening the foil packet.

Nutrition:

Calories: 381

Fat: 19

Fiber: 11

Carbs: 39

Protein: 48

PEACH PORK CHOPS

Intermediate | 30 minutes | Breakfast | 4 Servings

INGREDIENTS

- 1 pork chop
- 1 cup of peach preserves
- 1 tablespoon of butter, melted
- 1 teaspoon of balsamic vinegar

COOKING STEPS

1. Combine butter, peach preserves and vinegar and stir together.
2. Place pork chop on foil and coat with peach preserve mixture.
3. Wrap tightly in a foil packet.
4. Cook for 15 to 20 minutes, or until pork is cooked all the way through.
5. Remove from heat and let the packet sit for minutes before carefully opening it.

Nutrition:

Calories: 293

Fat: 16

Fiber: 11

Carbs: 23

Protein: 32

BLACK BEANS AND SAUSAGE

Intermediate | 45 minutes | Breakfast | 4 Servings

INGREDIENTS

- ½ pound of smoked sausage, sliced diagonally
- 1 can of black beans, drained and rinsed
- 1 carrot, peeled and diced
- 1 shallot, diced
- 1 garlic clove, minced
- 1 cup of chicken broth
- Salt and pepper, to taste

COOKING STEPS

1. Combine all ingredients in a foil packet.
2. Add salt and pepper, to taste.
3. Wrap foil packet up, leaving room for steam.
4. Cook for 30 to 35 minutes, or until carrots are soft.

Nutrition:

Calories: 259

Fat: 15

Fiber: 11

Carbs: 27

Protein: 38

LUNCH AND DINNER CAMPFIRE CHICKEN "STIR FRY"

Camp Master | 50 minutes | Breakfast | 4 Servings

INGREDIENTS

- 1 pound of boneless chicken breast, sliced thin
- 2 cups of green beans
- 2 cups of broccoli florets
- 1 ½ cup of red bell pepper, sliced
- 1 cup of onion, sliced
- 2 cups of cooked rice
- 1 tablespoon of sesame oil
- 2 tablespoons of soy sauce
- 1 cup of chicken broth
- 2 teaspoons of ground ginger
- 1 teaspoon of crushed red pepper flakes
- 1 teaspoon of garlic powder
- 1 teaspoon of salt
- 1 teaspoon of pepper
- 1 24"x24" or larger piece of greased aluminum foil

COOKING STEPS

1. Packet folding style: Tent

2. In a large bowl or plastic food bag, combine the chicken, green beans, broccoli florets, red bell pepper, and onion.

3. In a separate container, combine the sesame oil, soy sauce, chicken broth, ground ginger, crushed red pepper flakes, garlic powder, salt, and pepper.

4. Add the chicken and vegetable mixture to the aluminum foil. Top with the cooked rice, if desired. You could also eliminate the rice from the packet and heat it separately. Then add it to the dish when you're ready to eat.

5. Pour the sauce over the meat and vegetables.

6. Create a tent style fold and place the packet on your heat source.

7. Cook for 35-40 minutes, or until meat is cooked thoroughly and vegetables are crisp and tender.

Nutrition:

Calories: 421   Fat: 17   Fiber: 14   Carbs: 49   Protein: 43

TEX MEX CHICKEN POCKETS

Camp Master | 50 minutes | Breakfast | 4 Servings

INGREDIENTS

- 4 boneless chicken breasts, approximately 6-8 ounces each
- 1 15-ounce can white beans (or canned beans of choice)
- 2 cups of fresh corn kernels
- 1 cup of tomato, diced
- 1 cup of onion, diced
- 2 cups of Salsa Verde
- 1 teaspoon of cumin
- 1 teaspoon of cayenne powder
- 1 teaspoon of garlic powder
- 1 teaspoon of salt
- 2 cups of Monterey Jack cheese, shredded or cubed
- 4 12x12 or larger pieces of greased aluminum foil

COOKING STEPS

1. Packet folding style: Flat.
2. Add one chicken breast to each piece of aluminum foil.
3. In a separate bowl or container, combine the white beans, corn kernels, tomato, onion, and salsa verde. Mix well.
4. Season the chicken with cumin, cayenne powder, garlic powder, and salt.
5. Top each piece of chicken with the bean and salsa mixture.
6. Add ½ cup of cheese to each packet and create a flat style fold for each one.
7. Place packets onto your heat source and cook for 35-40 minutes, or until the chicken has reached an internal temperature of 165°F.

Nutrition:

Calories: 363 | Fat: 23 | Fiber: 17 | Carbs: 34 | Protein: 48

CHICKEN BREAST WITH SAVORY STONE FRUITS

Camp Master | 50 minutes | Breakfast | 4 Servings

INGREDIENTS

- 4 chicken breasts, 6-8 ounces each
- 1 cup of peaches, sliced
- 1 cup of cherries, pitted and sliced in half
- ½ cup of apricots, sliced
- 1 cup of red onion, sliced
- 2 cups of fresh spinach leaves, shredded
- 2 tablespoons of olive oil
- 1 tablespoon of cracked black pepper
- 2 teaspoons of thyme
- 1 teaspoon of rosemary
- 1 teaspoon of garlic powder
- 1 teaspoon of salt
- 4 12"x12" or larger pieces of greased aluminum foil

COOKING STEPS

1. Packet folding style: Tent.
2. Add one chicken breast to the center of each piece of aluminum foil.
3. In a separate bowl or container, combine the peaches, cherries, apricots, red onion, and spinach. Drizzle with olive oil and season the fruit with thyme, rosemary, garlic powder, and salt.
4. Mix well, breaking up the fruit slightly to release the juices.
5. Add equal amounts of the fruit mixture to each piece of chicken.
6. Create a tent style fold for each packet and add it to your heat source.
7. Cook for 35-40 minutes or until the internal temperature reaches 165°F.

Nutrition:

Calories: 290　　Fat: 18　　Fiber: 11　　Carbs: 40　　Protein: 26

BACON RANCH CHICKEN BAKE

Camp Master | **50 minutes** | **Breakfast** | **4 Servings**

INGREDIENTS

- 1 pound of boneless chicken breast, cubed
- ½ pound of bacon strips, diced
- 1 cup of red onion, sliced
- 1 cup of cherry tomatoes, cut in half
- 1 cup of sour cream
- 1 package of ranch dressing/seasoning mix
- 1 tablespoon of olive oil
- 1 18x18 or larger piece of greased aluminum foil

COOKING STEPS

1. Packet folding style: Flat
2. In a large bowl or bag, combine the chicken, bacon, red onion, and cherry tomatoes.
3. In a separate container, combine the sour cream and ranch dressing mix.
4. Drizzle the chicken and vegetables with olive oil and add the sour cream mixture.
5. Toss until chicken and vegetables are evenly coated.
6. Place all of the ingredients in the center of the aluminum foil and create a tent style fold.
7. Add to your heat source and cook for 35-40 minutes or until the chicken's temperature has reached 165°F.

Nutrition:

Calories: 273   Fat: 10   Fiber: 5   Carbs: 21   Protein: 29

CAJUN CHICKEN WINGS

Camp Master | 40 minutes | Breakfast | 4 Servings

INGREDIENTS

- 12 chicken wings
- 2 tablespoons of vegetable oil
- 2 tablespoons of Cajun seasoning
- 1 teaspoon of salt
- 1 teaspoon of pepper
- 1 lime, quartered
- 1 24"x24" or larger piece of greased aluminum foil

COOKING STEPS

1. Packet fold style: Flat.

2. In a bowl or other container, add the chicken wings, Cajun seasoning, salt, and pepper.

3. Transfer the wings to the center of the aluminum foil.

4. Dress the wings with freshly squeezed lime juice and add any remaining juice to the chicken.

5. Create a flat fold packet and add it to your heat source.

6. Cook for 25-30 minutes, or until chicken has reached a temperature of 165°F. Turn occasionally while cooking.

Nutrition:

Calories: 299   Fat: 18   Fiber: 6   Carbs: 17   Protein: 38

CAMPFIRE QUESADILLA

Camp Master	40 minutes	Breakfast	1 Servings

Cooking Method: Foil-wrapped and direct grilled

INGREDIENTS

- 1 flour tortilla
- ½ cup of Mexican blend cheese
- Any meats or veggies you'd like to add

COOKING STEPS

1. Place tortilla on a piece of foil.

2. Add cheese and other ingredients to the tortilla. Beef, chicken and shrimp are good meats to add. You can also add bell peppers, onions and mushrooms for a loaded quesadilla. Cook the meat and veggies in a skillet before placing them in the tortilla.

3. Fold both ends of the tortilla over one another.

4. Fold the aluminum foil over the top of the quesadilla.

5. Place the foil packet over direct heat and cook until the cheese is melted.

Nutrition:

Calories: 230   Fat: 9   Fiber: 3   Carbs: 17   Protein: 23

Chapter 14. Lunch and Dinner

JAMBALAYA FOIL PACKET

Beginner | 25 minutes | Lunch and Dinner | 4 Servings

INGREDIENTS

- 1lb/453g of Sausage (sliced)
- ½ Yellow onion (diced)
- 1 Red bell pepper (diced)
- 1 Green pepper (diced)
- 2 ribs celery (diced)
- 3 tbsp. of Cajun seasonings
- 1 cup of instant rice
- 1 cup of Water/Chicken broth

COOKING STEPS

1. In a large bowl or container, combine all ingredients.
2. Divide the mixture between 4 foil packets.
3. Place over the campfire and cook 20-25 minutes or until rice softens

Nutrition:

Calories: 349   Fat: 12   Fiber: 10   Carbs: 23   Protein: 19

BACON RANCH CHICKEN PACKET

Beginner   55 minutes   Lunch and Dinner   5 Servings

INGREDIENTS

- 6 tbsp. of Butter (melted)
- 2 tbsp. of Ranch seasoning powder
- Salt and pepper to taste
- 4 Chicken breasts
- 1lb/453g of Red potatoes (quartered or halved)
- 1 cup of Cheddar cheese (shredded)
- 4 slices of bacon (cooked and crumbled)
- 2 tbsp. of Parsley (chopped)

COOKING STEPS

1. In a small container or bowl combine butter, ranch seasoning, salt and pepper, and whisk thoroughly.

2. Drizzle potatoes in a bowl with ranch butter mixture and toss to coat evenly.

3. Place a chicken breast into each foil packet and season with salt and pepper.

4. Distribute potatoes evenly among foil packets.

5. Fold the edges and cook over a campfire for 30 minutes.

6. Sprinkle cooked ingredients with cheese and bake for a few additional minutes.

7. Before serving, make sure to sprinkle with bacon and parsley.

Nutrition:

Calories: 287   Fat: 10   Fiber: 3   Carbs: 13   Protein: 26

EASY BAKED FISH IN FOIL PACKETS

Beginner | 35 minutes | Lunch and Dinner | 2 Servings

INGREDIENTS

- 2 Whitefish fillets
- 1 tbsp. of Olive oil
- 2 tbsp. of Chives (chopped)
- 1 cup of Potato (diced)
- 2 cups of Vegetables of your choice (chopped)
- 2 tbsp. of Thyme
- 1 Lemon
- Salt and pepper to taste

COOKING STEPS

1. Prepare 2 separate foil packets.
2. In a bowl, container or Ziploc bag combine olive oil, herbs, and vegetables and mix well.
3. Drizzle the foil with a little bit of olive oil.
4. Distribute vegetables evenly between 2 foil packets.
5. Arrange one fish fillet on top of vegetables in each foil packet.
6. Sprinkle with lemon juice.
7. Bring two ends of foil together to close the packet and place over the campfire where you will bake fish and vegetables for 25 minutes or until fish is fully cooked through.
8. Serve straight in the foil and enjoy.

Nutrition:

Calories: 291 | Fat: 11 | Fiber: 9 | Carbs: 26 | Protein: 31

DAD'S QUICK AND EASY TRI-TIP

Intermediate Cooking Method	40 minutes	Lunch and Dinner	6/8 Servings
	Direct and indirect grilling		

INGREDIENTS

- 1 tri-tip
- 4 cloves of garlic, minced
- 1 teaspoon of black pepper
- 1 teaspoon of fresh lime juice
- 1 cup of olive oil
- 3 tablespoons of Pappy's seasoning

COOKING STEPS

1. Combine all marinade ingredients in a large freezer bag and shake until blended.

2. Place tri-tip in a bag and let marinate overnight.

3. Prepare grill for direct grilling.

4. Place the tri-tip on the grill over the coals and cook for 6 to 8 minutes on each side.

5. Move tri-tip to an area further away from the coals to complete grilling. Cook tri-tip for an additional 5 to 10 minutes on each side, depending on how done you want it to be.

6. Let the tri-tip sit for 8 to 10 minutes before slicing and serving it.

Nutrition:

Calories: 201   Fat: 9   Fiber: 5   Carbs: 19   Protein: 11

EASY BEER-BATTERED FISH FILLETS

Intermediate | 40 minutes | Lunch and Dinner | 8 Servings

Cooking Method: Cast iron skillet placed on grill over the campfire.

INGREDIENTS

- 8 fish fillets
- 8 lemon halves
- 2 cups of buttermilk pancake mix
- 2 cups of beer
- ½ cup of extra virgin olive oil
- Salt and vinegar, to taste

COOKING STEPS

1. Combine buttermilk pancake mix with beer and stir until mixed.

2. Place olive oil in cast iron skillet and place on grill over the campfire. You want to have the grill at the lowest possible setting. Let the olive oil heat up for 5 minutes.

3. Dip the fish fillets in the batter and drop them in the skillet. The oil has to be hot enough to fry the fish fillet, or the fillets won't properly cook.

4. Cook the fillets until golden brown on both sides.

5. Squeeze lemon over filets and garnish with salt and vinegar, to taste.

Nutrition:

Calories: 253   Fat: 16   Fiber: 7   Carbs: 22   Protein: 39

EASY OMELETS

Intermediate Cooking Method | 30 minutes Skillet on the campfire grill | Lunch and Dinner | 2 Servings

INGREDIENTS

- 3 eggs
- 3 strips bacon, cooked and crumbled.
- 3 sausage links, cooked and crumbled
- 10 sliced mushrooms
- Spinach, to your liking
- ½ cup cheddar cheese

COOKING STEPS

1. Add the 3 eggs to the skillet and stir them with a spatula.

2. Add the spinach and mushrooms and stir them into the eggs.

3. Spread the eggs out across the pan.

4. Let them cook for a few minutes and then add the bacon and sausage to the middle of the omelet.

5. Fold the eggs over the top of the bacon and sausage.

6. Sprinkle cheese on top and serve warm.

Nutrition:

Calories: 290 Fat: 19 Fiber: 12 Carbs: 29 Protein: 54

FOIL-WRAPPED BAKED POTATOES

Intermediate Cooking Method | 60 minutes Foil Wrapping | Lunch and Dinner | 1 Servings

INGREDIENTS

- 1 potato
- 1 tablespoon of butter
- Toppings (sour cream, chives, cheese, bacon bits, etc.)

COOKING STEPS

1. Cut a slit in the top of the potato and spread butter across the top.

2. Wrap potato in aluminum foil. Double-wrapping works best because it protects the potato from scorching.

3. Bury the potato in the coals of the fire.

4. Let it sit for 45 minutes to an hour, or until the potato is soft like a normal baked potato.

5. Let cool for 5 to 10 minutes and unwrap.

6. Top with your favorite toppings and enjoy.

Nutrition:

Calories: 299   Fat: 18   Fiber: 11   Carbs: 47   Protein: 25

FOIL-WRAPPED GROUND BEEF VEGGIE STEW

| Camp Master Cooking Method | 40 minutes Foil Wrapping | Lunch and Dinner | 1 Servings |

INGREDIENTS

- 1 large potato
- ½ medium onion, chopped
- ½ clove garlic, minced
- 3 tablespoons of crumbled bacon
- ¼ cup of cheddar cheese
- ¼ cup of mozzarella cheese
- 1 tablespoon of butter
- ½ teaspoon of sea salt
- ½ teaspoon of pepper

COOKING STEPS

1. Cut the potato into cubes.
2. Add all of the ingredients to a foil wrap and wrap it up tightly.
3. Place the foil wrap into the hot embers of your campfire for 15 to 20 minutes or until potatoes are cooked, and cheese is melted.
4. Let cool for 10 minutes and eat.

Nutrition:

Calories: 295   Fat: 20   Fiber: 10   Carbs: 37   Protein: 49

FOIL-WRAPPED GROUND BEEF VEGGIE STEW

| Camp Master Cooking Method | 25 minutes Skillet and Foil Wrapping | Lunch and Dinner | 1 Servings |

INGREDIENTS

- ½ pound of hamburger
- ½ cup of water
- 1 carrot, cut into coins
- ½ medium onion, diced
- 1 stick celery, chopped into small pieces
- ½ of clove garlic, minced
- 1 tablespoon of basil, chopped
- 1 can of cream of mushroom soup

COOKING STEPS

1. Brown hamburger in a skillet.
2. Make a cup out of aluminum foil.
3. Add all ingredients to the cup and stir up.
4. Fold aluminum foil over the top of the cup and place the cup directly in the hot embers of the fire.
5. Let cook for 15 minutes, or until veggies are cooked to your liking.
6. Let cool for 10 minutes and serve warm

Nutrition:

Calories: 278   Fat: 15   Fiber: 7   Carbs: 35   Protein: 21

FOIL-WRAPPED LEMON GARLIC FISH

Camp Master Cooking Method | 30 minutes Foil Wrapping | Lunch and Dinner | 1 Servings

INGREDIENTS

- 1 fish filet
- ¼ cup of water
- Half lemon
- 10 cherry tomatoes, halved
- 1 small garlic clove, minced
- ½ teaspoon of lemon salt
- Cracked black pepper, to taste

COOKING STEPS

1. Place fish in foil.
2. Squeeze the lemon over the fish.
3. Place cherry tomato halves around the fish.
4. Season with garlic, lemon salt, and cracked black pepper.
5. Add water and close foil wrap.
6. Place foil wrap directly into hot embers of the campfire.
7. Let cook for 15 to 20 minutes, or until fish is cooked all the way through and flaky.

Nutrition:

Calories: 267   Fat: 14   Fiber: 6   Carbs: 19   Protein: 42

FOIL-WRAPPED POPCORN

Camp Master Cooking Method | 40 minutes Foil Wrapping | Lunch and Dinner | 2/4 Servings

INGREDIENTS

- ¼ cup of popcorn
- 5 tablespoons of vegetable oil
- Salt and melted butter, to taste

COOKING STEPS

1. Place unpopped popcorn in the center of a large piece of foil.

2. Drizzle the oil over the popcorn.

3. Fold the edges of the foil up to the center. You're going to want to leave plenty of room for the popcorn to pop.

4. Make sure the edges are sealed and place the foil packet in the hot embers of the fire.

5. Let sit until the popcorn stops popping. It helps if you shake the packet from time to time.

6. Remove from fire and carefully open the packet. There will be a lot of hot steam inside, so be extremely careful.

7. Add butter and salt to your liking and enjoy.

Nutrition:

Calories: 207   Fat: 8   Fiber: 9   Carbs: 23   Protein: 11

Chapter 15. Snacks and Sides

MINI FRUIT PIES

Beginner | 20 minutes | Snacks and Sides | 4 Servings

INGREDIENTS

- ✓ 1 mini pie crust
- ✓ ½ can of fruit pie filling

COOKING STEPS

1. Place mini pie crust on the foil.
2. Fill pie crust with pie filling.
3. Wrap pie crust tightly with foil.
4. Place in the campfire. Make sure the crust stays upright, so the filling doesn't fall out.
5. Cook for 6 to 8 minutes, or until filling is hot all the way through.

Nutrition:

Calories: 197   Fat: 10   Fiber: 9   Carbs: 21   Protein: 18

NACHOS

Beginner | 25 minutes | Snacks and Sides | 4 Servings

INGREDIENTS

- 1 cup of tortilla chips
- 1 cup of shredded Mexican blend cheese
- ½ cup of refried beans
- Toppings (salsa, sour cream, jalapenos, etc.)

COOKING STEPS

1. Place the tortilla chips on the foil.
2. Place beans on chips and spread out.
3. Spread liberal amounts of cheese onto the chips.
4. Seal foil packet tightly. Poke a few holes in the top.
5. Cook for 10 to 12 minutes, or until the cheese is melted and the beans are hot.
6. Open the packet carefully and add toppings.
7. Serve hot.

Nutrition:

Calories: 232   Fat: 14   Fiber: 9   Carbs: 17   Protein: 29

ORANGE CARAMEL CINNAMON ROLLS

Beginner · 25 minutes · Snacks and Sides · 4 Servings

INGREDIENTS

- 1 orange
- 2 cinnamon rolls
- 2 tablespoons of caramel

COOKING STEPS

1. Cut the orange in half.
2. Scoop out the orange, so you have two hollow shells.
3. Place one cinnamon roll in each orange half.
4. Wrap in aluminum foil and place in the campfire.
5. Let cook for 10 to 15 minutes, or until cinnamon rolls start to brown.
6. Remove from fire and open foil packet.
7. Drizzle with caramel and eat while still warm.

Nutrition:

Calories: 246   Fat: 17   Fiber: 6   Carbs: 30   Protein: 19

ORANGE MUFFINS

Beginner | **25 minutes** | **Snacks and Sides** | **4 Servings**

INGREDIENTS

- ✓ 1 orange
- ✓ 1 package of instant muffin mix

COOKING STEPS

1. Make the instant muffins following the directions on the box.

2. Cut the orange in half and scoop out the meat. Leave the peel intact. When done, you should have 2 empty orange halves.

3. Fill each of the halves with a muffin mix.

4. Wrap each half in its own foil packet. Be careful to keep the orange peel upright, so the muffin mix doesn't spill out. Leave the top of the packet somewhat open to allow any steam that forms to escape.

5. Cook for 15 minutes, or until the muffin is cooked all the way through.

Nutrition:

Calories: 187 | Fat: 10 | Fiber: 9 | Carbs: 25 | Protein: 13

QUESADILLAS

Intermediate   20 minutes   Snacks and Sides   4 Servings

INGREDIENTS

- 1 flour tortilla
- ½ cup of shredded Mexican blend cheese

COOKING STEPS

1. Sprinkle cheese on a flour tortilla and fold it in half.

2. Place the tortilla on a piece of foil and wrap it up tightly.

3. Cook for 10 minutes. Flip the packet over after 5 minutes. Make sure cheese has melted before eating.

4. If you cook this recipe on a grill, you can get nice grill marks on your quesadilla if you leave it in one spot on the grill.

Nutrition:

Calories: 183   Fat: 9   Fiber: 4   Carbs: 15   Protein: 6

PEANUT BUTTER S'MORES TORTILLAS

Intermediate | 20 minutes | Snacks and Sides | 4 Servings

INGREDIENTS

- 1 flour tortilla
- 1 tablespoon of peanut butter
- Miniature marshmallows
- Chocolate chips

COOKING STEPS

1. Spread peanut butter on the tortilla.
2. Add as many marshmallows and chocolate chips as you want.
3. Roll the tortilla up like a burrito.
4. Wrap it in foil.
5. Cook for 6 to 8 minutes or until marshmallows and chocolate has melted.
6. Let cool for a few minutes, unwrap and enjoy.

Nutrition:

Calories: 249

Fat: 12

Fiber: 5

Carbs: 23

Protein: 19

WAFFLE CONE S'MORES

Intermediate | 20 minutes | Snacks and Sides | 4 Servings

INGREDIENTS

- 1 waffle cone
- Miniature marshmallows
- Chocolate chips
- Mini pretzels
- Peanut butter

COOKING STEPS

1. Fill a waffle cone with marshmallows, chocolate chips, mini-pretzels, and peanut butter.

2. Wrap tightly in foil.

3. Place in the campfire and cook for 6 to 8 minutes, or until chocolate is melted.

4. Unwrap carefully and let cool for a few minutes before eating.

Nutrition:

Calories: 237

Fat: 15

Fiber: 7

Carbs: 28

Protein: 11

COCKTAIL SAUSAGE WITH BACON AND MAPLE SYRUP

Intermediate	35 minutes	Snacks and Sides	4 Servings
Cooking Method	grill over campfire or camping propane/gas barbecue grill set on medium-high heat.	Equipment:	saucepan, cast iron skillet, wooden toothpicks

INGREDIENTS

- 1 cup of ketchup chili sauce
- 1 cup of maple syrup
- 24 ounces of cocktail sausage
- 1 pound of bacon, each strip sliced in half
- 1 tablespoon of vegetable oil

COOKING STEPS

1. Place a saucepan on the grill and add the ketchup chili sauce and half the maple syrup. Mix together and simmer for 5 minutes, stirring and watching that it won't get burned. Set aside.

2. Wrap each sausage with one half-strip bacon. Secure with a toothpick cut in half (optional).

3. Add oil to the cast iron pan. Place sausages seam side down on cast iron pan. Drizzle with remaining maple syrup and cook for 10-15 minutes, flipping until all bacon sides have been cooked and are golden brown.

4. To serve, use sauce made earlier as a dipping sauce.

Nutrition:

Calories: 252   Fat: 16   Fiber: 4   Carbs: 19   Protein: 32

PEANUT BUTTER S'MORES TORTILLAS

Camp Master	40 minutes	Snacks and Sides	4 Servings
Cooking Techniques	grill over campfire or camping propane/gas barbecue grill (set on medium-high).	Equipment	sealable plastic bag such as a zip lock bag, heavy-duty aluminum foil sheet.

INGREDIENTS

- 1 pound of Paneer cheese
- Cilantro or mint to serve

<u>Make-Ahead Marinade:</u>

- 5 tablespoons of plain yogurt
- 3 tablespoons of tandoori masala
- 1 tablespoon of lemon juice
- 2 cloves garlic, minced
- 1 small piece ginger, peeled and grated
- Olive oil
- Sea salt

COOKING STEPS

1. Cut Paneer into even cubes.

2. Mix all the marinade ingredients in a sealable bag like a ziplock. Put the Paneer into the marinade bag, and allow to rest for 1-2 hours in the cooler. Turn bag over a few times.

3. Place the Paneer cubes on an aluminum sheet, placed directly on the grill over the campfire hot coals for 4-5 minutes, turning periodically. Cook until lightly browned.

4. To serve, place on a plate and sprinkle with herbs.

Nutrition:

Calories: 239   Fat: 12   Fiber: 4   Carbs: 16   Protein: 35

EASY CORN BREAD SKILLET

Camp Master	35 minutes	Snacks and Sides	6/8 Servings
Cooking Techniques	grill over campfire or camping propane/gas barbecue grill (set on medium-high heat.).	Equipment	large iron cast skillet.

INGREDIENTS

- 3 tablespoons of butter
- 2 cups of yellow cornmeal
- 1 teaspoon of baking powder
- ½ teaspoon of baking soda
- ½ teaspoon of salt
- 1 large egg, lightly beaten
- 2 tablespoons of honey
- 1½ cups of buttermilk or whole milk

COOKING STEPS

1. Put butter in a cast iron pan. Place on the grill over the campfire until the butter melts. Remove from the fire with oven mitts and set aside.

2. Mix all the rest of the ingredients in a large bowl. Whisk vigorously until the batter is smooth and lump-free.

3. Pour batter into a hot cast-iron skillet. Place it back on the campfire's grill, cover and cook until golden brown and springy to touch, roughly 20-25 minutes. To make sure the cornbread is ready; insert a toothpick or a pointy knife that comes out clean. If some wet batter is visible, continue cooking for a few

minutes.

4. To serve, cut into slices and offer honey or butter to top the warm cornbread.

Nutrition:

Calories: 229 Fat: 13 Fiber: 5 Carbs: 38 Protein: 10

TERIYAKI CHICKEN SKEWERS

Camp Master	18 minutes	Snacks and Sides	6 Servings
Cooking Techniques	grill over campfire or camping propane/gas barbecue grill (set on medium-high heat.).	Equipment	wooden skewers, soaked for at least 30 minutes in water, heavy-duty aluminum foil.

INGREDIENTS

- 1 10-ounce bottle of Teriyaki sauce, preferably reduced sugar
- ¼ cup of sesame oil
- 2 garlic cloves, minced
- ¼ cup of lemon juice
- 1 tablespoon of honey
- 2 pounds of boneless and skinless chicken breasts, cut into half-inch strips

COOKING STEPS

1. Mix the ingredients for the marinade together in a sealable bag. Add chicken strips. Close the bag, and let sit for 1 hour in the cooler. Turn the bag over 2-3 times for a perfect coating of the chicken.

2. Place each chicken strip onto a skewer. Place the skewers on an aluminum foil sheet placed on the grill over the campfire hot coals. Watching carefully, allow to cook 6-8 minutes on each side, turning only once. If you want some grill marks, cook directly on the grill, but watch carefully as the sugary marinade tends to burn easily.

Nutrition:

Calories: 259   Fat: 19   Fiber: 9   Carbs: 21   Protein: 49

GRILLED BREAD WITH HERB BUTTER

Camp Master	20 minutes	Snacks and Sides	1 Servings
Cooking Techniques	grill over campfire or camping propane/gas barbecue grill (set on medium-high heat, direct-fire cooking.).	Equipment	small saucepan, grilling forks

INGREDIENTS

- 1 stick butter (½ cup)
- 2 garlic cloves, minced
- ½ cup of fresh parsley, finely chopped
- ½ tablespoon of dry chives (or 1 tablespoon of fresh minced chives)
- 1 loaf crusted country-style bread, sliced thick

COOKING STEPS

1. Place butter in a small saucepan on the grill over the lowest heat. Keep away from the center of the fire. Add garlic and chives. When melted, remove from heat and add parsley.

2. Brush one side of each bread slice with herbed butter. Grill butter side down over coals for about 2 minutes, until golden brown.

Nutrition:

Calories: 201   Fat: 12   Fiber: 4   Carbs: 16   Protein: 19

Chapter 16. Desserts and Drinks

GRILLED PINEAPPLE WITH CINNAMON SUGAR

Beginner | 15 minutes | Desserts and Drinks | 4/6 Servings

INGREDIENTS

- 1 cup of brown sugar
- 2 teaspoons of ground cinnamon
- 1 pineapple, cut, cored, sliced into 6 wedges

COOKING STEPS

1. Mix the sugar and cinnamon and pour into a sealable bag. Add the pineapple wedges, seal the bag, and shake. Make certain each piece is coated well.

2. Place the pineapple pieces directly on the grill. Cook for 3-5 minutes a side, until the sugar melts, and there are nice grilling marks on the pineapple.

Nutrition:

Calories: 208 Fat: 9 Fiber: 8 Carbs: 17 Protein: 12

BANANA CHOCOLATE SURPRISES

| Beginner | 15 minutes | Desserts and Drinks | 4 Servings |

INGREDIENTS

- 5 bananas, unpeeled
- 1¾ cup of semi-sweet chocolate chips (mini M&M and other chocolate candies can also be used)
- Coconut flakes
- Mini marshmallows

COOKING STEPS

1. Cut each banana down its inner center, leaving the peel on. Open each banana carefully and just wide enough to insert some filling. Stuff each banana with chocolate chips, coconut flakes, and mini marshmallows. Wrap each banana in tin foil, and place it on the fire.

2. Let them cook for about 5 minutes. Allow banana to soften and chocolate chips to melt sufficiently. Test one of the bananas to see if it's cooked enough.

3. To serve, carefully open the packet. Remove some of the peel to form a large enough opening, and then eat the stuffed banana with a spoon directly in the packet.

Nutrition:

Calories: 227   Fat: 14   Fiber: 4   Carbs: 19   Protein: 11

STRAWBERRY SHORTCAKE

Intermediate | 15 minutes | Desserts and Drinks | 8 Servings

INGREDIENTS

- ½ cup of honey
- 1 can of biscuit dough
- ½ cup of cream cheese, softened
- 1 cup of strawberries, sliced

COOKING STEPS

1. Prepare the campfire.
2. Grease both sides of the pie iron with butter, vegetable oil, or cooking spray.
3. Cut the biscuit dough in half.
4. Place one-half at the bottom of the pie iron. Spread with 1 tablespoon of cream cheese.
5. Add 1 tablespoon of honey and sliced strawberries.
6. Place the other dough half on top and press the edges together to seal.
7. Close and latch the pie iron.
8. Place the pie iron over the coals and cook for about 2 minutes. Flip and cook for 2 minutes more.
9. Remove the pie iron from the coals. Serve warm.

Nutrition:

Calories: 541 | Fat: 25 | Fiber: 5 | Carbs: 71 | Protein: 11

CAMP COOKIES

Intermediate | 25 minutes | Desserts and Drinks | 8 Servings

INGREDIENTS

- ✓ Sugar Cookie Dough Pillsbury
- ✓ Butter, vegetable oil, or cooking spray

COOKING STEPS

1. Prepare the campfire.

2. Grease both sides of the pie iron with butter, vegetable oil, or cooking spray.

3. Add 2 tablespoons of cookie dough to the bottom of the pie iron. Press down gently. Repeat on the other side of the pie iron.

4. Without closing it, place the pie iron over the coals and cook for about 12 minutes until the cookies are slightly golden on the edges.

5. Remove the pie iron from the coals. Repeat with the remaining dough. Serve warm.

Nutrition:

Calories: 170 | Fat: 9 | Fiber: 5 | Carbs: 22 | Protein: 2

LEMON OR CHOCOLATE DESSERT PIE

Intermediate | 35 minutes | Desserts and Drinks | 4 Servings

INGREDIENTS

- 2 slices white bread
- Lemon Meringue Pie
- 4 white marshmallows
- 1 tablespoon of Lemon curd
- Chocolate Caramel Pie
- Lindt milk chocolate balls, halved
- 2 tablespoons of caramel spread

COOKING STEPS

1. Prepare the campfire.
2. Grease both sides of the pie iron with butter, vegetable oil, or cooking spray.
3. Place one slice of bread at the bottom of the pie iron. Add the lemon pie or chocolate pie ingredients one by one.
4. Place another slice of bread on top. Cut off the edges.
5. Close and latch the pie iron.
6. Place the pie iron over the coals and cook on both sides until evenly golden brown.
7. Remove the pie iron from the coals. Serve warm.

Nutrition:

Calories: 610   Fat: 23   Fiber: 5   Carbs: 100   Protein: 5

CAMPFIRE BANANA BOATS

Camp Master | 15 minutes | Desserts and Drinks | 1 banana boat

INGREDIENTS

- 1 Banana
- 2 tbsp. of chopped chocolate
- 8 mini marshmallows
- 1 square of graham cracker

COOKING STEPS

1. Take a banana and cut it down the middle with the peel still on. Not all the way through, just on the other hand, before the edge of the knife grazes the peel. Push somewhat apart from the peel and banana.

2. Stuff the banana with chocolate and marshmallows in the middle.

3. Cover the foil around the banana. Put on a campfire or barbecue for around 10 minutes before the fillings have melted, and the banana has cooked.

4. Unwrap the banana with a smashed graham cracker and tip. Serve and enjoy.

Nutrition:

Calories: 224　　Fat: 12　　Fiber: 5　　Carbs: 15　　Protein: 5

GRILLED PEACHES WITH YOGURT, HONEY, AND MINT

| Camp Master | 20 minutes | Desserts and Drinks | 12 Servings |

INGREDIENTS

- 2 large fresh peaches
- 1 tbsp. of brown sugar
- 1 or 5.3 oz of Thick yogurt or vanilla-like Greek yogurt or Skier of about
- 3 or 4 minced leaves of mint

COOKING STEPS

1. Cut the peaches in two halves, and the pits are extracted. Sprinkle over the sliced sides with the brown sugar.

2. Put the side-cut peaches on the grill on low to medium or low heat and cook until the peaches are cooked and start to soften around 8 minutes. Cover each half of peach with vanilla yogurt, a drizzle of sugar, a pinch of mint, and remove it from the grill. Serve and Enjoy.

Nutrition:

Calories: 240   Fat: 7   Fiber: 4   Carbs: 12   Protein: 12

CAMPFIRE APPLE CRISP

Camp Master | 30 minutes | Desserts and Drinks | 2 Servings

INGREDIENTS

- 2 or 3 apples, 1/4" thin-sliced.
- Oil or butter for 1 tbsp.
- 1 tbsp. of cinnamon, ground
- 1/2 tbsp. of Nutmeg, ground
- 1/2 tbsp. of cloves, ground
- 2 tbsp. of Bourbon
- 1/4 cup of brown sugar
- 1 cup of granola

COOKING STEPS

1. In an 8' or 10' cast iron pan, sauté the sliced apples over medium heat in a bit of oil or butter until they tend to soften, around 5 minutes.

2. Mix the bourbon, spices, and sugar, stir. Proceed to simmer for 5-10 minutes before the sauce become thick, and the apples are soft. Sprinkle the granola uniformly over the top after removing it from heat. Straight from the pan or serve with a large scoop of coconut ice cream in individual bowls!

Nutrition:

Calories: 150 | Fat: 5 | Fiber: 4 | Carbs: 2 | Protein: 3

AUTUMN PLUM SKILLET TART

Camp Master | 60 minutes | Desserts and Drinks | 4 Servings

INGREDIENTS

- ✓ 1 cup of flour, plain
- ✓ Salt
- ✓ 4 tbsp. of grated butter
- ✓ 2-3 cups of ice water
- ✓ 4-5 ripe black plums
- ✓ 2 tbsp. of sugar coconut
- ✓ 1/3 cup of water
- ✓ 2 tbsp. of honey

COOKING STEPS

1. Break the plums into wedges and place part of the coconut sugar and water in a saucepan.

2. Carry to a boil and cook over the campfire, stirring to avoid sticking as necessary, adding more water if necessary (but the plums should begin to release moisture as they cook).

3. Add the liquid into another pan until the plum becomes soft; save it for Plum & Rosemary Prosecco Spritz to make syrup.

4. Unroll the baking sheet and lay it in a pan, and cut it into the edges. Place the plum bits, set in one flat sheet, into the skillet. Drizzle with the honey and gently fold the corners.

5. Cover with aluminum foil or lid, and then cook until the edges begin to become brown on low heat.

Nutrition:

Calories: 240 | Fat: 7 | Fiber: 4 | Carbs: 12 | Protein: 12

Conclusion

Camping is an adventurous and essential outdoor ritual for many, a dreamlike natural phenomenon that has served as the centerpiece of backwoods gatherings for centuries. Your relaxation and desire to love your trip to the fullest degree will significantly influence how you prepare for camping and what kind of recipes you follow to make your trip even more memorable. Hence, this is a comprehensive guide for camp survival and healthy food. We hope this book could be a real friend and encourage you to come up with your very own inventive modifications.

Camping can be a life-changing experience, and done right it might as well be the most memorable one. Remember that camping in the wild is no easy task, especially if this is your first time, though reality TV might want you to believe otherwise. You can never be too prepared, so plan well and in advance. Research your campsite well and make sure you check and double-check your lists so that you don't overlook important things. The absence of a small plastic bag can pose a huge challenge once you are away from civilization. Talk to a few fellow campers—see what tips and tricks they use and try to adapt them.

You should plan every single meal that you are going to prepare and be sure of your skill if you can do it or not. Plan every meal and each snack of your camping trip to guarantee that you don't burn through your food or get caught consuming breakfast chips on the first night. Depending on how you're camping (i.e., backpacking through the wilderness or RV camping), how that plan will look will vary greatly. You should be able to bring enough equipment to make meals as you would in your kitchen if you're camping in a car or RV.

If you are willing to cook chicken or beef on your camping trip, it is better to marinate your meat beforehand. You should do it before you leave for camping. Other than that, you should have the proper tools and utensils for the meals you are going to prepare. The right equipment is something you must be careful about. When it comes to a cooler, pack it wisely!

GOODLUCK!

Made in the USA
Monee, IL
29 May 2021